UTPAL DUTT

Born in 1929 in Barishal (now in Bangladesh), Utpal Dutt began his theatrical career in college at St Xavier's, Calcutta, playing in selected scenes from *Romeo and Juliet*, *Macbeth* and *Richard III*. In 1947, he found his 'guru'—Geoffrey Kendal, and his life with the strolling Kendals lasted 'from August 1947 to the end of 1948, and again from February 1953 to the end of 1954'. Dutt's first significant directorial experiment was a modern-dress version of *Julius Caesar* in 1949, for the group Amateur Shakespeareans. This group was later renamed Little Theatre Group in 1950, and moved to productions in Bengali. Real popular success came with *Angar* in 1959 at Minerva (taken on a 'long lease' in 1959), followed by *Angar*, *Ferari Fouj*, *Titash* and *Kallol*. *Kallol* made a savage criticism of the Congress, the party in power in 1965, and Dutt was immediately arrested and detained in Presidency Jail without trial. Released in March 1966, he did a series of documentary plays at Minerva and joined the Naxalite movement, going underground in 1967. Arrested in Bombay in 1968, when he turned up for the shooting of *The Guru*, he was finally released on the intervention of his American producers. In the 1968–69 season, he took up his first assignment in the Jatra and went on to write and direct *Rifle*. Between 1968 and 1972, he wrote and directed 17 Jatra plays. Wanting to explore the form further, he formed the Vivek Jatra Samaj (for rural and suburban audiences) and People's Little Theatre for the urban proscenium. PLT survived and it was the immediate success of its *Tiner Talwar* in 1971 that ensured a second run for Dutt. PLT went on to deliver more hits, including *Barricade* (1972) and *Duswapner Nagari* (1974).

Dutt was also acquiring a reputation as a film actor, both in Calcutta and in Bombay. Major performances include either lead or supporting roles in films like Satyajit Ray's *Jana Aranya* (The Middleman) and *Agantuk* (The Stranger); Mrinal Sen's *Bhuvan Shome* and *Chorus*; and James Ivory's *Shakespearewallah* and *The Guru*.

A prolific writer, he has left behind a vast quantity of writings on theatre, literature and cinema as well as the monographs *Towards A Revolutionary Theatre*, *Shakespeare-er Samaj Chetona* and *Girish Manash*.

Recipient of the National Award for Best Actor in *Bhuvan Shome* in 1970 and a Fellow of the Sangeet Natak Akademi (1990), Dutt died in 1993.

On Theatre

UTPAL DUTT

LONDON NEW YORK CALCUTTA

Seagull Books, 2009

First printing, 2009
Second printing, 2022

ISBN 978 8 1 7046 251 4

British Library Cataloguing-in-Publication Data
A catalogue record for this book is available from the British Library

Typeset by Seagull Books, Calcutta, India
Printed and bound by Hyam Enterprises, Calcutta, India

Contents

What Is to Be Done? 1

Theatre and Ideology 37

Innovation and Experimentation in Theatre 53

OVERVIEWS/REVIEWS/REPORTS/COMMENTS

Shakespeare and the Modern Stage 64

Oedipus Wrecked 73

The Calcutta Stage 79

Sartre's Choice 85

Little Theatricals 88

Death of a Salesman 92

Mythmakers 98

Shakespeare and Coffee 102

Cues 107

Euler of the Theatre 111

The Indian Kulturkampf 116

O Blood! Blood! Blood!
(*Othello*, Act III, Scene 3, Line 455) 121

More Things in Shakespeare 126

THEATRE NOTES

Why Classics? 132

Soliloquy 135

Line Rhythm in Theatre 138

Jatra and Its Relevance 151

What Is to Be Done?

When I first received an invitation to speak here, I thought that either I was mad or that the organizers were. Nobody asks me to speak in surroundings such as these. Moreover, this is too polite, too gentlemanly a gathering to be addressed by me. I do not usually speak and write in English. I will very often make ghastly mistakes—please forgive me and bear with me. I speak out in the street corners before our plays go on. We have this thing called the street-corner play during which we scream at the audience because there are no mikes. The police does not permit the use of mikes on street corners, so we shout at them and shout things which are vicious. These are sometimes funny but more often they are extremely loaded—so much so that a section of the audience does not laugh; they are hurt. So, I am afraid I am going to make a mess of this speech. It is going to be published, which means it must be written and I have never delivered a speech that has been written. Anyway, I will try my best to be as polite as I can.

The name of this series of lectures is 'What is to be done?' 'What is to be done?' is the name Lenin gave to his celebrated work on the degenerating influence of economism on the proletarian movement. 'Economism' requires explanation. There was this great movement in Europe, the European Proletarian Movement—a socialist movement by and of the people who said that increasing wages for the workers was the only way to socialism, that workers should be fighting for their bonuses, for their wages, and not for state power. It took a Lenin to come and correct these mistakes. Higher bonuses are all right, he said; higher wages are all right, but they are not everything; they are not all. Not until state power is captured by the proletariat will the proletariat rest. These mistakes of economism and the errors that the ideological wing of the Bolshevik Party was making, in surrendering to the bourgeois propaganda and accepting certain aspects of this propaganda as if there were no alternatives, were analysed by Lenin in his work. *Pravda* and other newspapers of the Bolshevik Party were not fighting back—not answering these charges of the bourgeoisie as they should have done. So 'What is to be done?' was written. Therefore, economism, according to Lenin, is the influence of the bourgeoisie within the proletariat. The proletariat can always arrive at the truth that a few rupees more in his daily wage are essential for him. It does not require a political party like the Bolsheviks to tell him that—to explain that to him. What Lenin demanded of the Bolshevik Party, of the intelligentsia, of his newspapers, was that they should go and explain to the workers what they have learnt already from this society, what they have obtained—the advantages of this society. They have been educated, so they must bring politics to the workers, not economism—not salary increases or a bonuses of a few roubles. He demanded that they bring politics to the masses, to the proletariat. So economism was an influence of the bourgeoisie within the proletarian movement.

In the same way, and this is why I borrow the name, I propose to talk of the political theatre in our country—its tasks and the various means the ruling class adopts to corrupt and deflect it from its goal. There will be no attempt to address those who consider the theatre a 'pure' art, who love it for its own sake. They rather remind me of those rich young men in affluent countries who seek to relieve their boredom with drugs. I do not think we can afford such expenses in a country like India, where 40 per cent of the masses still do not receive two square meals a day. Such irresponsible young theatre-workers, who make a virtue of their irresponsibility, bring to mind the Czarist duchess in St Petersburg who was a great lover of opera—she wept with the heroine night after night while her footmen froze to death outside on the street. I think we can do without such a homicidal love of art.

Political theatre wages a struggle for the minds of men. In any society, the ideas of the ruling class dominate the society as a whole. It is the ideas of the ruling class in India today which are passed off as 'eternal Indian values' and other wonderful notions. Unconsciously, we accept them as eternal Indian culture, eternal Indian art. But, actually, it is only because the bourgeoisie order us to do so. It is in the bourgeois class interest that such arts, art forms, values and cultures are promoted. They require these for survival—survival as a class. But they present them in such a manner that their ideas prevail, and the other classes begin to accept them as true. There is nothing eternal about them, nor are they specifically Indian. If we analyse them, we shall find them to be random and incoherent, ideas gathered from all over the world to justify the exploitation and robbery which sustain the ruling class and defend it against challenges from the ruled. Take the Congress centenary speeches in Bombay. Listening to them you would imagine non-violence to be a specifically Indian concoction thought up by Mahatma Gandhi from ancient Indian books, and that whatever the Indian government does today is automatically non-violent, even if it is war with Pakistan or army actions in Amritsar. It is always the enemy who is violent; the Indian is always like the benign Buddha. But there is nothing characteristically Indian at all about non-violence. The Irish used it for three centuries against English imperialism and Gandhi freely adapted an idea from Leo Tolstoy. Yet non-violence must be paraded as typically Indian to spread a smoke-screen over the appalling violence of the Indian bourgeoisie and landlords, and to disarm the masses so that they do not resist, revolt or take up arms. It is one of the ideological weapons of the ruling class to enslave the minds of men.

Political theatre is one of our weapons against theirs—one of our ideological weapons. While the ideas of the ruling class seek to emasculate the masses, to lead them like sheep to the slaughter, political theatre seeks to awaken their consciousness, their awareness and militancy. While the ruling class falsifies Indian history and seeks to show that India has always been non-violent, political theatre rediscovers the true historical facts and proves that violence has been the midwife of all social change in the past and will continue to be so in the future. The political theatre tries to restore to the masses their revolutionary traditions and exposes non-violence for what it is today—a hypocritical mask to hide the hideous face of the ruling class.

For example, the story of India's freedom struggle continues to be mangled by the authorities in order to eliminate from it all reference to armed struggle. They have managed to practically wipe out, for example, the great peasant rebellions of the eighteenth century, the one known as the great Sannyasi-Fakir Rebellion, which shook the East India Company's government. They have practically suppressed the epic revolt of 1857, but for a ritualistic mention of the Rani of Jhansi. (She has become too well known to be suppressed altogether.) They never refer, for example, to the Mysore Wars of Hyder Ali and Tipu Sultan, where English arms were brought to disgraceful defeat; they have banished from Indian history the battle of Chilianwala and the patriotic struggle of the Sikhs. The struggle of the Marathas is never mentioned either. In their version of the Indian freedom movement, the armed martyrs of the 1905 struggle in Bengal do not exist, nor do Bhagat Singh and the Punjab revolutionaries, nor does the 1946 RIN Mutiny in Bombay nor Subhas Chandra Bose and the INA. This entire side of the Indian freedom struggle is sought to be wiped out. In fact, to them the 200-year-old struggle for India's freedom is reduced to one word—Gandhi, whether Mahatma, Mrs or Rajiv. Falsification of history cannot go to more shameless lengths. History, after all, is a process and the British decision to quit India was the result of the cumulative force of thousands of men, most of them armed, fighting through the years, dying on the battlefield or on the gallows. To reduce all that to the black magic of one name, or to claim that India won freedom because one man wove khadi, or drank goat's milk, is not just ignorance or stupidity (they are not so ignorant nor so stupid) but a deliberate attempt to obliterate the long tradition of mass armed struggle, to prevent that tradition from exerting any influence on the present-day behaviour of the masses.

The climax of this propaganda storm is the film *Gandhi* (1982) directed by an Englishman who is so careful to protect English honour that he spends a lot of footage on the supposedly historical court martial of Brigadier General Dyer, the butcher of Jallianwalla Bagh. Indignant English officers grill him for his cruelty and impress upon modern Indian audiences the imperialists' sense of justice and fair play. In actual history, of course, the English bourgeoisie raised a fund of £80,000 for Dyer and held meetings throughout England, congratulating him for his decisiveness and initiative; there was no court martial. Such lies abound in *Gandhi*, where you never see a cruel English officer—all the beating, kicking and burning alive are done by Indians to Indians. Englishmen appear in the film only as well-wishers of Gandhi, and the message comes through, clear and precise, that it took the genius of Englishmen to recognize the genius of Gandhi. And it is they who made him known to the world. Of course, they put him in prison many times but that was merely to make him famous.

The Indian authorities bore the financial burden of this imperialist extravaganza—naturally, it suits their purpose to have such a Gandhi. And Reagan's USA thought it necessary to help out with as many Oscars as it could salvage from the other claimants. That merely shows up the film's obsequiousness, how useful it can be in the hands of imperialism. The racist South African regime wanted the film shown all over their country, and Sir Richard Attenborough was ready to go to South Africa, to a segregated cinema, if you please, to preside over the première. Only a vociferous protest from the Blacks and Asians in South Africa, and a judicious threat from a Swapo guerilla group, daunted Sir Richard's enthusiasm.

How is it that the philosophy of Gandhi, who began his struggle in racist South Africa, now gives aid and comfort to South African racists and becomes an attack on the struggling Blacks in South Africa? How is it that Gandhi is welcomed by the barbaric White minority in South Africa, and the African National Congress, founded by Gandhi, threatens to bomb it? The reason is simple. The bourgeoisie have been at work here. They have turned Gandhi into their Trojan Horse to help infiltrate the revolutionary strongholds of the world—whether it is Nicaragua or South Africa—and disrupt the philosophy of armed resistance from within.

That alone explains the shower of Oscars in the USA at a time when the audiences are busy applauding the rapes and murders of Rambo. Rambo is their ideal. Kill and rape—that is the ideal they hold up before young Americans; kill and rape without compunction. In the latest Rambo film, he is a Vietnam veteran who says, 'We lost there because we did not kill gooks enough.' Now, placed next to him by these awards of Oscars is Gandhi, the apostle of Attenborough's peace. This is the US imperialists' ideal wish to place before Vietnam, Nicaragua, the rebels of El Salvador and the Blacks of South Africa: follow Gandhi and give up arms, so this time we *can* kill gooks enough and win.

There has always been a dearth of heroes in the capitalist world. Not to speak of the charisma of a Che Guevara or a Nelson Mandela, they have nothing to compare even with Ortega or the tame and meek Desmond Tutu. So now Attenborough has tried to provide one with his version of a moth-eaten Gandhi, one who will be always be more attractive to the colonized than the Reagans and Schultzes in their uniform grey business suits.

Political theatre in this country was supposed to retaliate with dozens of historical plays, rediscovering the history of anti-imperialist armed struggles. Whether it be the uprising of Santhal tribesmen in Chhotanagpur, or the martyrdom of Birsa Bhagwan (as his name suggests, Birsa is now worshipped in the Munda villages of Bihar as a god), the people of this country everywhere worship armed martyrs. In the evenings, they light lamps at the graves of unknown warriors. People composed songs to Rani Lakshmibai, to Babu Kunwar Singh of Jagdishpur, to Nana Saheb of Bithoor, to Kshudiram Bose of Bengal. That is the way of oppressed people the world over. They sang to John Brown in America, to Joe Hill, and about how the treacherous sheriff shot down the Dalton brothers. They sang to Granwail in Ireland, to McSweeney, and about how Lucy Rose was hanged at dawn. Everyone knows these songs.

To think of a song rising from the people's heart on, for example, the Gandhi–Irwin talks, or the Mountbatten mission or our beloved MPs who are talking at midnight about the Gujarat reservation issue, is patently absurd. People generally sing of one who has died fighting—as a sacrificial lamb, as a Jesus Christ—by way of an atonement for the indifference of the community.

Historical plays about the anti-imperialist struggle were one sure way of not only hitting back at the distortion of history by the ruling class but also of quickly uniting with the masses. Heaven knows we need the masses in our theatres. Many of us are anaemic from the absence of an audience. Many political theatres have been reduced to barren intellectual gymnastics in empty city halls. Many of us keep complaining that there are no plays in this country. If we study recent history, we will find so many themes dear to the masses (and discover how the companies did not wait for people to come to the theatre, but took theatre to the people). We too can have an endless repertoire of plays and perform them before packed houses.

Of late, our theatre-workers have turned to the villages, not to look for themes for political folk songs or subjects for new plays but to collect a song here and a dance there and then drag those performers to the city and add those bits to whatever old play they are doing. This is supposed to be 'using folk forms in theatre'. Often, those songs and dances do not go at all with the play upon which they are grafted; they jar and throw the play out of gear. But it still must be done, because that is the current fashion—you must use folk elements in your theatre even if it ruins your play and destroys the folk.

Let there be an end to this kind of city fad. You cannot master a folk form by glancing at it for a day or two. And unless we have mastered it thoroughly, we cannot use it. That is the object of opening your theatre to folk influences. Folk elements must be so integrated that they enrich theatre. They will not enrich theatre but destroy it if bits of them are thrown in, piecemeal.

But this propaganda continues. In every sphere of life, every minute of every day, the propaganda machine—the media—of the ruling class is turning out masses of lies and dangerous ideas. Their films, for example, which now dominate every corner of the country, peddle reactionary ideas as a factory turns out goods. What are the principal lessons they seek to foist on the masses and which we should fight against by means of political theatre?

1. The hero is the final arbiter of justice and the fist is the primary argument. We never find the masses in action in commercial films. They grovel on the ground before Mr Amitabh Bachchan, for example, and appeal to him to save them, whereupon he takes a submachine gun or uses his fists and puts everything to right. The bourgeois is always a fascist at heart. He glorifies the almighty hero because in politics he would much rather have a Mussolini ruling this country. Indira or Rajiv Gandhi are not brutal enough for him. The popularity of such films is as great a danger to this country, as Rambo is to the peace of the world. Sylvester Stallone's Rambo, whose rapes and murders on the screen are cheered by audiences in USA, is used as a model by the cheap B-grade actor who is now their President, which means he wants to rape. That is one of their methods of brutalizing the great American people and preparing their minds for a nuclear war. And Indian films

glorifying the brutal hero who yells *insaaf main karunga* ['I shall bring justice'] similarly divert the people's minds from paths of mass agitation, strike and insurrection, to plain gangsterism or a patient wait for a messiah. They undermine the people's self-confidence and make them look for a saviour, a super hooligan, who will appear one day, probably in New Delhi. What was Hitler after all but a super hooligan?

2. The obnoxious use of women in films is another constant exercise in the bourgeois concept of Indian society. When they are not making women dance naked for the edification of sex-starved males, they are making them snivel and kiss the feet of their husbands in a sickening display of wifely virtue and loyalty. That is supposed to be the Indian tradition, you see—an ancient Indian virtue that women lick the feet that kick them. Perhaps bride-burning will soon be consecrated as a sacred Indian custom—who knows?! To restrict the minds of men to the steel frame of feudal backwardness, to deny them enlightenment, to give them false pride in a society that is rotten to the core—that seems to be the subject of such films. So that wife-beaters can be proud of their deeds.
3. Then, of course, there is a steady outpouring of films that unashamedly peddle superstition and show the futility of rational thought. I mean stuff like *Jai Santoshi Maa* (1975). They discover new mothers constantly from the dungheap of discarded local cults and give them a new, all-India lease of life.

Of course, against this trend is the new democratic thought—experimental films made by brave filmmakers. But they are swamped by the power of tycoons, the publicity machine, the monopoly on distribution, the denial of outlets and a thousand other gangster methods of capitalism.

Take Doordarshan, that other great weapon of the ruling class. It has been entirely handed over to the bourgeoisie in exchange for hard cash, and the mindless morons who constitute the Indian bourgeoisie have brought the TV programmes down to their own level. A play after all is not a play to them but a vehicle to advertise shampoo or soap, again with naked women bathing in springs or running around, swinging their tresses from side to side. We have no programme that is not sponsored by some Shylock or the other; and we even expect our beloved prime minister's next telecast speech to be sponsored by the makers of a particular brand of boot polish. It is but natural, only natural—and there is no use losing our tempers about it—that the bourgeoisie will ultimately dominate every channel of mass communication.

Take the language they have invented especially for TV and radio. The Mughals in India delighted in speaking Persian, knowing that the masses did not understand it; the English spoke English for the same reason. The present rulers have gone after Hindi with a knife, excising every word of Urdu, Persian or Arabic origin (even though that word may be understood all over India), and replaced it with something concocted from a Sanskrit dictionary. The result is a news broadcast which no one but Benares pundits understand. '*Ab aap hindi mein samachar suniye*', *wo bolte hain aajkal. Bolna chahiye*, '*ab aap samachar mein hindi suniye*.' ['Now listen to the news in Hindi': is what they say these days. Instead, they should say: 'Now listen to the Hindi in the news.'] That would make more sense. For example, replacing a word like *zaroorat*. The word *zaroorat* has entered every single Indian language from Bengali to Marathi. It is, however, being replaced with something called *avshyakta*. This is a kind of vandalism that takes one's breath away. And often, due to imperfect education, Sanskrit words are wrongly used. For example, *varjit* is now being used widely to denote 'prohibited'. It means nothing of the sort. In Sanskrit it means 'abandoned'—from *varjan*. The Sanskrit for 'prohibited' should be *nishedh* or *nishiddh*. Anyway, what is the object of setting a bunch of half-educated clerks to massacring a beautiful and simple language such as Hindustani? What is the reason behind this madness? The ruling class, all over the world and throughout history, wishes to create an esoteric language of its own, from French spoken by the Normans in England to the use of Latin by the Church for nearly 15 centuries. It clothes the rulers in mystery and denies the masses the right to understand statecraft. It also makes mass illiteracy permanent, which is what the rulers probably desire. And the Indian rulers describe this destruction of Hindi as the restoration of an ancient tradition, as if our rishis in their forests spoke like our TV newscasters.

Thus their vague insistence on a 'link language'—whatever that might mean for India—not only wilfully obstructs the growth of other languages but destroys Hindi itself. It makes Hindi a barren grammatical exercise, not spoken by anyone in the country. A language grows only by being spoken by millions and by borrowing from other languages—consciously and unconsciously. Far from uniting the country, this idiotic bastardization of Sanskrit is rapidly disuniting it. If the ruling class really wanted a lingua franca in India, they could have easily found it—current, alive and vital in the Hindi that India's railway workers, for example, have been speaking for a hundred years now. That language may not conform to Sanskrit grammar but it is beautiful to the ear and easy to pick up, with masses of English, Tamil and Telugu words freely taken over. Take the dialect Sadri, spoken by the tea-garden workers in Bengal and Assam; it is predominantly

Hindi, with numerous words from Santhal and Oraon. Tea gardens teem with workers from all over India and they have never had any difficulty in communicating with one another. A common language evolves out of common labour, out of common economic compulsions; it cannot be wished into existence by fanaticism.

But the Indian ruling classes have no interest in the unity of the people of India; they merely wish to preserve the geographical unity of this country so that they can exploit it better, carry raw material to and fro to their factories and have a unified market for their products. The human factor, the cultural factor, the question of various nations who must have the right to develop their own language and culture to the full, is utterly repugnant to the ruling class. They equate such desire with separatism. Anything that does not promise immediate profit is dangerous and subversive to them. Their unity is a unity of exploitation. They are afraid of the unity of the exploited.

They have brought the country to a dreadful pass with their suppression of the various people's rights to self-expression. They do not hesitate to play off Haryana against the Punjab, or disenfranchise 23 lakh people in Assam. They rob the states of their wealth to strengthen their capital, and order the army out to shoot, burn and pillage wherever the people demand a fair share of their own wealth. They want New Delhi to be a dreaded name throughout the country. It is obvious that the bourgeoisie and the landlords will not preserve India's unity—they themselves are the greatest threat to it. It was they who created Bhindranwale to fight the Akalis, and it is they who have handed over power to the worst chauvinists in Assam. We must remember that the Indian bourgeois divided the country once before, and, without any hesitation, drowned it in the blood of Hindus, Muslims and Sikhs, merely to somehow get into the saddle of power. Talk of the country's integrity from such arch-traitors is laughable, to say the least. Add to this their vast machinery of the press, printing white lies every day, honouring our prime minister's silliest remarks as if they were the pronouncements of a great statesman, unleashing a barrage of untruths to pass off his notorious 'accords' as the dawn of peace in this country, turning the rulers' blatant attempts to dismember the country into their opposite, into a struggle to preserve its unity. An assessment of this massive cultural offensive launched by the bourgeoisie is necessary before we can even begin to talk of what is to be done by the political theatre-workers today.

THE CONCEPT OF TRUTH

There is a fashion among critics and a few playwrights to demand absolute, impartial truth in plays. No matter what *they* write, whenever *we* write a play we have to be absolutely truthful. They charge us with distorting historical facts. For example, they once attacked us, accusing us of deviating from the truth, in our play *Kallol* (The Wave, 1965). In *Kallol,* the rebel cruiser *Khyber* refused to surrender in spite of air-attacks by British RAF bombers, whereas, in history, *Khyber* had actually surrendered after the second air-raid. Unhistorical, they screamed. Distortion of truth!

But, you see, we do not believe in absolute truth at all. Truth is always class truth. There are always at least two truths involved in every issue: the truth of the bourgeoisie and the truth of the proletariat. To the bourgeois, the *Khyber* surrendered. *Khyber* was the name of the cruiser which fought a desperate battle during the 1946 Naval Mutiny in Bombay. When the British finally started bombing this cruiser out at sea, it surrendered. But in our play we showed that it did not. It went on fighting the air-force, and screaming, 'We will not surrender!' This is the point of contention. To the bourgeois, the surrender of the *Khyber* is the end of the Mutiny and that is that. To the proletariat, the surrender of the *Khyber* is the beginning of a long process of freedom struggle, one that continues. Therefore, whereas a newspaper can afford merely to report that the *Khyber* has surrendered, a political play cannot. That the *Khyber* surrendered is merely a fact, not the truth. The truth includes the historical process that the *Khyber* unleashed. The bourgeois insists that you report only what you see, only what is. Both Maxim Gorky and Bertolt Brecht insist that our truth embraces not only what is but what will be, or should be. For the same reason, Eisenstein's famous rebel ship *Potemkin* does not surrender at the end of the film, though history records that it did.

Is this distortion of history? Certainly not. On the contrary, this portrayal alone honours history, because the defiance of the battleship *Potemkin* portends the Russian Revolution of 1917. If the film had ended with *Potemkin*'s abject surrender, the audience's attention would not have been drawn to the historical process—merely to an incident which is insignificant by itself. And Eisenstein has been able to reach the truth behind the fact precisely because he is partisan—not neutral. Thus, paradoxically, only by being partisan can one be really truthful. The neutral, uninvolved, dispassionate investigator often ends up by being a liar or, worse, an advocate of the bourgeois view of life.

Political theatre all over the world has this great advantage over the bourgeoisie: that it draws sustenance from the philosophy of Marx and Engels; that it views all phenomena of nature as interconnected; that it does not analyse an incident in isolation but connects it to a historical process. In short, it has a proletarian philosophy as a guide.

Why is it that the proletariat unerringly arrives at the truth and the bourgeois, with his retinue of hired writers and hack-philosophers, swims among unanswered questions, fantasizes about reality, produces endless new schools of thought from McLuhan to the semi-

Marxist Frankfürt school, and keeps returning to God and religion in some form or other? The American Marxist Fredric Jameson answers this question beautifully: it is because the bourgeois has leisure to contemplate and speculate, but his world is full of crises, losses and depressions. It is because of this that he expresses his insecurity in self-contradictory thought. The worker has been deprived of leisure to think and this has saved him from the dangers of abstract thought. What can be viewed as a disaster for the proletariat (that he has no time at all to sit down and think), has also this advantage that he has no time to think abstract thoughts. The worker feels himself as part of production, as a moment in the process of production, and hence the sound materialist base of his philosophy. Thus Fredric Jameson on the American Marxist.

The worker himself is part of the production process; he feels himself as a moment in production; to him, the truth of capitalist society becomes obvious by the very fact that he is alive. Political theatre seeks to connect the various petty frauds, lies, deceptions and violences of the ruling class to the historical process, to its terror of extinction, its dread of the masses, to its inevitable dissolution. Even if the subject of our play is a single incident, we see it as part of the mosaic of history. And we must not be afraid to tackle that class's most well-guarded secrets, its tacit taboos, its most sensitive areas, as Rolf Hochhuth did in Europe by taking up the pope's collaboration in the massacre of the Jews in his play *Der Stellvertreter* (The Deputy, 1963). It is a massive play, nine hours long if played in full, documenting the pope's collaboration with Hitler. This obviously brought the house down, because he had touched the most sensitive area of the bourgeoisie—the greatest taboo of all—religion. He had hit at the Catholic Church and called it a collaborator with Hitler. But, in our country, our political theatre is so timid! Because we are afraid, of course—we have faced so much in the past, we have gone to prison, we have been bombed. So the most controversial issues in our country, at any moment, are left alone by our playwrights. To take some examples: the questions that agitate the people's minds most are the questions we must tackle first. We expect our Punjabi playwrights to write of Operation Bluestar and ask the most devastating questions. Why was no action taken when Bhindranwale turned a temple into a fort? Was not Mr Rajiv Gandhi one of Bhindranwale's most ardent patrons? Why was the Golden Temple attacked on Guru Arjun Jayanti when it was packed with pilgrims? How many were shot in the courtyard after surrender? Why was the library burnt? Ask and ask, until they squirm. Drive the knife in and turn it. That is how a political playwright conscious of his duty should think.

That is an example of what is to be done—take those questions which the rulers shy away from and turn them into a public debate. It is our task to involve the masses in these questions because they concern them most; they concern the security of their country, and no two-bit Doon School-type or a petty subaltern of the army has the right to keep these questions away from them.

DAY 2

Yesterday, we talked about the predominance of the bourgeois culture in our country and how the bourgeoisie managed to make all other classes accept that culture as their own. We were talking about eternal Indian values or, rather, bourgeois values which are not particularly eternal and certainly not Indian. No values or ideas are eternal—they keep changing all the time. Today we will begin with a discussion on alienation, one of the fundamental pillars of Marxist philosophy. Many bourgeois philosophers have taken up this question as if they invented it, as if they have discovered this truth. But, as early as 1844, Karl Marx in his *Economic and Philosophical Manuscripts* gave us the first detailed description of what he meant by the term alienation—*entäusserung* in German.

THE THEORY OF ALIENATION

Every theatre-worker must take into account the all-pervasive alienation of men in any society based on private property. Marx, in his *Manuscripts*, showed conclusively how, in a society where the fruits of labour belong to someone else, all men are increasingly alienated from other men and themselves. Man loses his faculties of love, mercy, enjoyment of beauty—all these being replaced by the single urge of acquisitiveness. He is also alienated from his past, from his language, from his heritage. In short, he increasingly becomes a spiritual lumpen, soon losing the ability to concentrate for any length of time on any artistic problem. The idiot-box in our time and the comics are an eloquent testimony to Marx's foresight, though neither existed in his age. Both wish to spare the consumer the trouble of thinking; they seek to provide a substitute for reading but without its attendant labour.

The phenomenon has, inevitably, invaded our country too, led and directed by our gangster bourgeoise. Any theatre-worker anywhere in this country can bear witness to the difficulty he faces in capturing the initial attention of his audience with any serious theme. Even 10 years ago the problem was not so acute; 10 years hence the problem will be 10 times worse.

For example, about 10 or more years ago, some time in 1954–55, we did a Bengali translation of *Macbeth* and it was an instant hit in the villages of Bengal. The villagers found the story exciting with all its witches, ghosts, duels, fights and battles. They were ready to accept all this along with all of the Shakespearean philosophy; they were interested in all the long soliloquies too. In 1972, we revived *Macbeth*.

This time we did no more than 10 performances and withdrew it—the first time we stoppped after a hundred—for we felt that the audience was not listening at all. They were in no mood to listen to the sound of poetry for any length of time, nor to labour and discover its meaning—that was too much for them; they were too exhausted, too weary. I suppose that would be the experience of any theatre group anywhere in this country.

Many of our theatre-workers, despairing of making themselves heard, switch over to pointless farces and thus hope to capture an audience. They soon realize that three farces in a row are just as boring to an alienated audience as is *Hamlet*. Others experiment with form, seeking to rouse interest with songs, dances, acrobatics, mime and what-have-you. There was even a brief movement in the USA which sought to blame it all on the words, the text, and thus drove the spoken word out of the theatre and replaced it with well-chosen groans and screams. This automatically meant the rejection of the whole of the world's dramaturgy, from Sophocles and Shakespeare to Brecht and Lorca. According to them, all that was bad drama because it depended on words. And they believed in the creation of a new poetry—'Pregnant Noise'—whatever that may have meant. Whether it meant the noise made by pregnant women or noise pregnant with meaning, I do not know. But that is what they said: 'Creation of a new poetry of Pregnant Noise'. The result was dramatic!—the audience immediately awoke from their sense of alienation to a sense of deprivation and drove the actors out of the theatre.

We must remember that our playwrights and producers are themselves alienated individuals, and their wild experiments are totally alienated efforts. They do not transcend the alienation, but perpetuate it. James Joyce tried it in literature with his syntax and the coining of portmanteau words; Schoenberg tried it in music with his dissonance and deliberate ugliness of phrasing. Neither reached a mass audience, and merely festered within a coterie of intellectual admirers. Theatre cannot, by definition, be restricted to a coterie of intellectuals; if the masses do not flock to it, it need not exist at all.

So now what is to be done about form? There are theatre groups whose admirable seriousness of purpose and very commendable enthusiasm in presenting political theatre end in such soporific productions that half the audience falls asleep, and the other half walks out, vowing never to return. This is admitted. It happens to me too. These groups fail to take into account the importance of form as a method of waking up a weary audience. Brecht openly said that he aimed at periodically astounding the audience (he used the German word *erstaunen*) to break down this alienation. There has to be an artistic use of sensation on the stage. You manipulate the form to create a sensational effect, so that the audience wakes up—at least it does not go to sleep—and listens to you.

But if these efforts to astound, to rouse the audience, are mere jugglery, mere stunts unrelated to the cultural roots of the audience from which the playwright is alienated, they will not rouse the audience but irritate it. Experiments in form should evolve from that tradition of folk culture from which the bourgeois tries to sever the masses. Theatrical experiment should evolve from that past which lies dormant in the audience's memory. Brecht declares that he derives his inspiration from the Bible and that his poetry is a derivation of Martin Luther's translation of the same. Unashamedly, he declares that he found his inspiration in the deepest tradition of the Christian peoples of Europe. He raked the whole of mankind's memory to find idioms for his form, including Canton opera; never did he experiment in a vacuum. A fine example of true theatrical experiment in our country is perhaps Jabbar Patel's production of *Ghashiram Kotwal*

(Vijay Tendulkar, 1972), using Maratha folk traditions and Natyasangeet in a brilliant effort to conquer the minds of a modern audience. All successful experiments in modern theatre have somehow struck a chord of reminiscence in the audience, have helped the audience overcome a bit of its alienation and given back to it a part of its heritage.

To counter this, the bourgeoisie everywhere, especially in India, has begun a worship of pristine, pure folk drama, to be reproduced exactly as it was played a few centuries ago—the slightest deviation considered sacrilegious. It sponsors several groups and individuals who are high priests of this folk worship and who love to rediscover lost folk forms—living folk forms put them off. If a folk form has evolved with time and survived, they hate it. How dare it move with the times and change? How dare it survive and not wait patiently to be revived, rediscovered? How dare it not die? It is obvious that any folk form which has died did so because it refused to change. Therefore to now bring it on stage in its primitive unchanged form is not to revive it, but to seal its doom and bury the corpse. It is obvious that folk theatre contains much feudal filth: songs, skits and dances added to please the drunken lord who was its patron. The cry for 'pure' folk is a cry for a revival of this filth, for a rediscovery of such gems of obscenity for today's audiences.

These folk experts, financed by the bourgeoisie, are actually trying to disrupt the solid work already done by the Indian People's Theatre Association (IPTA) in the 1940s and 50s. Political theatre's interest in the folk is primarily for its form, certainly not for its content. That form must be used for defiantly modern political content. That is why political theatre has used the Jatra form, for example, in Bengal; taking up its epic form and infusing it with anti-imperialist content during the British rule. The manuscripts seized and burnt by the police at that time are incalculable. Political theatre-workers in the Jatra today are using the form for plays on Lenin, Mao Zedong and Ho Chi Minh. P. L. Deshpande uses the form of the Tamasha similarly, for contemporary political satire which makes mincemeat of the rulers in New Delhi. The vast popularity of these experiments in Maharashtra and Bengal, and the involvement of the audience during performances, clearly show that experiments, which draw from folk forms but are not slaves to them, can break down the wall of alienation and rouse the audience.

We come to the next question of the bourgeois concept of drama, which, after all, is the fundamental point we are trying to make.

THE BOURGEOIS CONCEPT OF DRAMA

The bourgeois is essentially an enemy of the theatre, because he is a puritan. One must not forget that when the bourgeoisie first captured political power after the English Civil War, one of its first targets was the theatre. It suppressed theatre. Indiscriminately. While it dare not proceed to such extremes in this century, its hostility to the theatre manifests itself in other ways.

In Europe, critics and hack-writers set up a veritable howl against classical drama, charging it with 'exaggerated action', 'unreal characters' and 'excessive emotion'. All these three are quotations. Voltaire, the ideologue of the bourgeois democratic revolution, called Shakespeare a barbarian for the violence in his plays. Shaw could not stand Shakespeare either, nor could Tolstoy. None of them could not tolerate the absence of morals in his plays. In other words, they expected drama to be moral tracts on conjugal love and other insipid subjects; and when they found Othello going mad with jealousy and strangling his wife, they were outraged. To them, drama was a Sunday sermon preached by a right reverend to a strictly middle-class congregation, with all proprieties observed and appearances preserved. They, of course, know very well that at least half the husbands in the congregation, would on getting home, immediately get drunk and almost strangle their wives. But bourgeois morality consists mainly in keeping up appearances of gentility; and Shakespeare, unaware of this bourgeois code, refused to restrict himself to appearances and instead explored the depths of emotions, creating a veritable storm of unashamed and conflicting human beings fighting one another. To bourgeois critics this is barbaric, unrealistic; its class interests demand that such powerful emotions be denied. Such violence rocks the boat of bourgeois tranquility too much. The bourgeois wishes to believe that the capitalist world order is eternal. Shakespeare's drama disturbs that belief.

Northrop Frye, critic and bourgeois par excellence, solemnly notes that people today wish to see events in drama that can well happen in their own lives. How wonderful! People want to see events that can happen in the life of a petty bourgeois? Nothing happens—except an occasional flutter over a death in the family—say of an old man of 87 who dies of a heart-attack. He is not even killed, to provide some dramatic action. No, he dies of heart failure. So Frye actually tries to restrict drama to coffee-cups and breakfast, to a game of bridge and the one drink for the road. Anything bigger than that frightens him. Karl Marx, in his *The Eighteenth Brumaire of Louis Napoleon* (1852), somewhat playfully hits the nail on the head when he notes that the petty-bourgeois writers are almost like shopkeepers—they too cannot cross those limits in the mental world that the shopkeepers cannot in their daily business. The shopkeeper is a proverbial devotee of law and order. Disorder in any form—be it a strike, a procession, even the threat of one—immediately affects his business. It is this blind search for law and order that made the shopkeepers of Germany vote en masse for Hitler in 1933.

Similarly, the petty-bourgeois writers of Europe descended on the theatre with a shopkeeper's view of life—everything must be kept under control and there must be an inexorable logic behind all human behaviour. Unexpected and unforseeable behaviour—as in Shakespeare—endangers their class interest. They want human beings ticketed and numbered like puppets. They want dwarfs as heroes, not Hamlets and Macbeths. Their petty-shopkeeper world wants all human endeavour and violence to be compressed into a drawing-room format; therefore, unfathomable rages and passions are unrealistic to them. Generations of bourgeois critics brand *Hamlet* a problem play (as you know, it is a tradition in English criticism to brand *Hamlet* a problem play), because Shakespeare has failed to explain Hamlet's behaviour; there is no logic behind most of Hamlet's acts. Which means Shakespeare was a very bad playwright—he could not make the motive clear. They would never dare say Shakespeare was a bad playwright—because the whole world says he was the greatest, ever—so they keep saying that *Hamlet* is a problem play. Many others are problem plays too—*Troilus and Cressida*, for example. They have found many others, but Hamlet is the principal one. For example, here is the king praying and there Hamlet finds him. Hamlet is about to kill him. He raises his sword and then he does not kill him. He says that if he kills the king now (when he is praying), he will go to heaven. So he won't kill him now but some other time—when the king is drunk or is in his incestuous bed, so that he goes to hell. Modern critics who are oblivious of the religious beliefs of the Protestant or the Catholic Church during Shakespeare's time did not know that Shakespeare might well have believed that if you kill an enemy during prayer then he would go straight to heaven. So it won't be revenge but your enemy's salvation. It is because Shakespeare was a bad playwright that he could not explain why Hamlet did not kill his uncle. He goes on and on, finding various justifications for his delay, but he doesn't kill him. So this they attribute to William Shakespeare's weakness—there is no motive, after all, for Hamlet delaying the murder of his uncle. They forget that Shakespeare might have been trying to discover a motive for the murder, for the delay, none of which are clear to even Hamlet himself. They do not like this kind of a character, half of which is clothed in mystery and the rest hidden away in the complex of human behaviour. This they don't like because it might open up terrible possibilities in the actual social world which they rule. What do they actually mean when they brand *Hamlet* a problem play and say that Hamlet's motives weren't clear? They mean that the human psyche has been thoroughly mapped out already, that Hamlet cannot and should not act from motives that are unclear even to himself; that all the nooks and corners of the human mind have already been laid bare, and that anyone who discovers further depths to the human soul is unrealistic. This is the demand they make of playwrights, of no less a playwright than Shakespeare.

And so came the long era of drawing-room sets, of a lighting scheme trying to imitate a European twilight and dwarfs moving among them in predetermined patterns. These sets—called realistic by the bourgeoisie—were a ridiculous imitation of reality; vulgar and gaudy, they were an artistic disaster. It is shameful that, in the early 1860s, the Thèâtre Libre in Paris, darlings of the bourgeoisie, hung their sets with real hunks of beef and mutton to represent a butchershop. To this had they reduced the European theatre of Shakespeare. The plays are static, because the set-less empty space of the stage projecting into the auditorium of the classical theatre had been replaced by these horrible drawing rooms. The principle characteristic of classical theatre was that there was a huge space in which the actor had room to move, and in which you could imagine him moving from scene to scene. And he only said, 'Here we are, in the front of the castle,' and we imagined we were before the castle. 'Now let us go to battle' and the very next dialogue said, 'Here is the battle.' So the play moved dynamically from scene to scene, from place to place and the action was continuous—it was dynamic theatre. Then they replaced all that, and built a little toy-set drawing room. You could no longer, as in *Macbeth*, begin with a blasted heath and swiftly move to several parts of the battle and on to the Castle of Inverness in the space of one act. No. You were bound by the tinsel of the realistic set. Drama's mobility was gone.

And the dwarfs who came on stage and spoke realistic everyday street language drove poetry out of the theatre. The bourgeois does not understand poetry and is therefore suspicious of it. In his concept of realism, only the mundane slang of the marketplace or the stock exchange has any relevance. And that little box set he calls a middle-class drawing room precludes the possibility of anyone suddenly standing up and soliloquizing 'To be or not to be.' That would look and sound absurd. And violent action would be ridiculous in such a setting. In a middle-class drawing room, you don't draw a rapier and rush at your enemy. You may fume within, but it is forbidden to explode. You may be annoyed, but not angry. You may disapprove, but never condemn. You may love someone, with bourgeois proprieties observed, but you are not allowed to break into the Capulets' monument and kill yourself before Juliet's corpse. Such violent mad actions, such mad violence, are not permitted in a drawing-room set. These things are just not done—not done in bourgeois society, therefore not done in the theatre either.

Even those revolutionary writers who swore eternal hostility to the capitalist order, Ibsen and Shaw, could not break away from the bourgeois concept of drama—the static set, the insignificant men and women—and thus never fully realized their potential. Ibsen, for example, almost broke away at least twice—in *Peer Gynt* (1876) and in

Emperor and the Galilean (1873)—and tried to create a classical theatre using poetry and a kind of classical structure that reminds one of Shakespeare more than anything else. All the same, they did not permit it. He had fallen among Ibsenites—Ibsen himself was not an Ibsenite but he had fallen among Ibsenites who forced him to be their prophet. They wrote about how Ibsen was the prophet of this new middle-class movement in drama, how he was their greatest playwright and by and by he began to consent to it. 'My plays will live,' said Ibsen, 'and some day they will say I don't belong.' He was much larger than those petty playwrights.

Karl Marx, commenting on Lilo's *The Merchant of London* (1731), a typical bourgeois play and a very popular one in the early nineteenth century, said the bourgeois wants his hero to be a miser who deposits a part of his earning regularly in the savings bank. That is his concept of a hero. Of course he must save a part of his income, invest it in a savings bank, use it to create more money. Money wasted is not tolerated in bourgeois society. Who is the biggest waster of all? Hamlet, of course. This prince, studying at the university, comes back and finds his father murdered and refuses to go back to college. So he is a 'dropout', in our modern language. He drops out wilfully, decides not to live like his mother or uncle and dresses in black—a parallel of today's rebel clothing, long hair, army green or colourful clothes—and walks around the country looking like a beaten flower boy. Hamlet was but the beginning of that which has now become a cult. Hamlet was the first glimpse of a rebel inside society. He lived in society but was not of it, did not belong to it. So they couldn't stand him. Because, as Marx says, their model hero is a miser. He is a man who saves money, a man who is very careful with his expenses. Only such a man is dear to the bourgeoisie. Bourgeois theatre glorifies the virtues of bourgeois miserliness, thrift, puritanism, a dread of everything artistic. And teetotalism—half of the plays of the early nineteenth century in Europe had heroes who had never touched a drop of drink, because the bourgeois himself advocated teetotalism. There are reasons for it, historical reasons. The bourgeois, before he comes to power, watches the feudals, their licentiousness, their drinking, their womanizing, and acquires a kind of puritanic attitude to life, to all this excess. These middle-class dramas were full of heroes who were teetotalers. In countless bourgeois plays, the hero does not touch alcohol because it would be a waste of money. The bourgeios does not spend unless there is a return in cash. The commonest villain in these plays is the bohemian music teacher, somehow invariably Italian and who naturally drags a man down to womanizing and drinking. English plays are full of Italian villains. They would not call an English gentleman a villain. The music teacher must be Italian, because associating with music and the arts will naturally turn a man to womanizing and drinking. The Italian is an alcoholic and will always try to make love to the daughter of the house.

From Shakespeare to Lilo, that is the history of the bourgeois domination in the theatre. It should be noted that every attempt at experiment in the European theatre, from Adolf Appia to Bertolt Brecht was, in fact, a revolt against these bourgeois chains. The box-set, the static style of writing, in short the whole hocus-pocus of bourgeois realism.

Take just one case—characterization. The bourgeois insists that a beggar must be represented as a beggar, nothing else. You show him as we expect to see him. Don't shock us with something radically unexpected. You are obliged to restrict yourself completely to our experience of a beggar. But the beggar can be tomorrow's guerilla fighter. The Marxist accepts this. Man changes. But if you include this vision in your portrayal, you will be condemned as unrealistic. As happened to Gorky. When Gorky in his *Lower Depths* (1902) portrayed the hobo, the vagabond Satin, not as the bourgeois saw him every day but as a philosopher singing the praise of man almost in the same language as Hamlet, the outcry against such 'untruth' was universal in the bourgeois press. Gorky was almost hounded out of the theatre. He had violated their great taboo; he had discovered a humanist poet in a vagabond and time-waster. To challenge the bourgeois and declare that man is not a fully analysed quantity, that undiscovered aspects of his personality exist within him, that he is not a dissectable corpse, is almost blasphemous to the bourgeois. It opens up possibilities of dark forces of destruction, undetected and undetectable, within masses of men who may one day overthrow the bourgeois social order.

We too had a rich classical theatre in many parts of the country. It is being attacked. These attacks have just begun, from the thirties of this century, by a battery of intellectuals in Calcutta and Bombay who find nothing of note in our classical theatre tradition and which they accuse of 'melodrama'. That one word shatters every play. Whenever they try to analyse a play, they begin by saying, 'It is very melodramatic', which is actually a euphemism for 'unrealistic'. This was done by the bourgeois critics in Europe. Who can be more melodramatic than Shakespeare? There is no playwright in the world who can come within miles of Shakespeare in melodramatic effects, melodramatic action. Melodrama, after all, is a relative term. On the walls of Elsinore, even the ghost appearing before Hamlet and swearing him to vengeance is not melodramatic. But, of course, if your ideas of the theatre wallow in a middle-class drawing room, anything more assertive than 'Good morning' and 'Thank you' will appear melodramatic. Our classical theatre usually dealt with subjects from the Mahabharata, where Bhimsen drinks the blood of his adversary on the battlefield. Is that melodrama? I don't think so. In that terrifying fratricidal war, even that appears perfectly normal and inevitable. He has already sworn to drink the blood of the enemy. People actually wait for the moment when he will do so, because he swore it in the palace of the Kauravas when they were insulting Draupadi. But the intellectuals of our country keep pouring scorn and venom on the old theatre. And our young theatre-workers have been so influenced by these ignorant writings that they positively refuse to read old plays, mainly on the plea that they deal with mythology, with kings and princes.

Writing about kings and princes does not preclude the exploration of the human mind. Mythology is a poetic summary of an entire people's experience and is any day better material for drama than barren middle-class life. The Indian masses have been nurtured on epics and myths and would respond far more readily to today's social and political truths if they were presented in the grand style of an Indian epic. Our theatre should re-discover its heritage, its links with the classical Indian tradition, and learn from its supra-real epic style if it seriously intends to reach a mass audience.

WHAT IS TO BE DONE?

In order to re-establish an epic-style theatre, we must, first of all, rid the stage of those frivolous structures called box sets; they may be good enough for serial-style middle-class comedies on TV but anything bigger just does not fit there. Let us free the broad expanse of the stage for our heroes and villains to stride upon. I am not an advocate of acting before a black curtain but a firm believer in the use of sets in a dynamic manner, not as a fixed background to the actors but sets that participate in the action, sets that do not imitate reality but are defiantly non-representational. It is now almost forgotten that the hanging scenes were not originally painted to represent gardens, interiors and so on, to be changed surreptitiously behind closed curtains, but that they rose and fell before the audience's eyes at dramatic moments and were painted with clown's faces, a silver streak representing lightning, and, perhaps, a massive white death's head on a black field. That was the purpose of the painted scenes in Renaissance Italy as well as the Peking Opera. It is often forgotten that the revolving disc was not invented to change sets but to make the set itself revolve before the audience to emphasize a dramatic point. All this seemed unrealistic to the bourgeois realists. How can rooms revolve? Why should a painted mountain suddenly descend upon an actor? Gone was all metaphorical thinking from the theatre. Literal stupidity came to hold sway for 200 years. Dramatic imagination and poetic symbolism were shunned. Anything that violated photographic naturalism was considered unrealistic.

We have been experimenting for some years now with theatrecraft as it was before the bourgeoisie destroyed its dynamism, and we are happy to report some significant success. Modern audiences are no longer imprisoned by bourgeois prejudices. They do not question the propriety of painted scenes nor regard the revolving disc as interfering with the action of a play. On the contrary, they express their appreciation with cheers as they are suddenly and pleasantly struck by this unusual behaviour of what has always been deadwood at the back of the stage. These manipulations of stagecraft serve the same purpose as Brecht's *erstaunen* theory—they both help to end the audience's alienation.

In our play *Mahavidroha* (The Great Rebellion, 1973), we try to portray the Delhi episode of the 1857 war. We use nothing on stage except a big white canopy, operated by lines, which assumes various shapes right before the audience's eyes—a hill, a tent, an undulating field. In the scene where the sepoys of Meerut burst into premature mutiny, the canopy ceases to represent anything but flutters up and down in response to the call for revenge upon the white officers. In the scene at the Red Fort, where the rebellious sepoys arrive to force the feeble Emperor Bahadur Shah to assume leadership of the war, the text requires the emperor to be finally made to give *darshan* to the assembled multitude. We set up the window on the side, on the edge of the disc. As the reluctant emperor begins to walk to it, we turn the disc and the window swings around down-centre, framing the emperor. This heightens the emotional appeal of the 70-year-old infirm Bahadur Shah facing his patriotic subjects and swearing to lead them to battle.

The theatre, as we know it today, was originally imported from Europe but is now an accepted Indian medium. There have been some cries raised for a true 'Indian' theatre, whatever that may mean. Perhaps a reconstruction of the theatre as it was practised in Kalidasa's time? This is patently absurd. No one knows what the theatre was in Kalidasa's time, and, if we were to reconstruct it somehow, it would instantly send a modern alienated audience to sleep. The European theatre is here to stay, just as all art forms of the world are coming closer and closer to one another. This European theatre has a lot of potential, if we can do away with the trivialities inflicted by the upstart bourgeoisie.

But, to use the theatre, we must master its craft. We must trace the history of every part of it—the proscenium, the trapdoors, the apron, the cyclorama, the teasers, the painted scene, the constructed set, the curtain—and find out how and why it was used. Only then can we proceed to make experimental use of all these elements. Similarly, we must know the steps by which lighting was gradually introduced; lights were restricted by the bourgeois realists merely to making visible the action on the stage. Appia gave it a dramatic function, a dynamic role in intensifying drama. Extensive study of period Indian costumes and the principles of colour-schemes must be undertaken. All this mastered, the young *régisseur* is ready to experiment.

But so many of our young enthusiasts rush in where angels fear to tread. They begin too early to pose as iconoclasts in the theatre. They wish to break down without knowing what it is that binds them. They rush at walls without testing their own strengths and weaknesses. They wish to break the laws of the theatre without realizing that you need not break any of them but use them at will for various effects. The basic laws of the theatre have endured through centuries. The trick is to rediscover their mobility, their vitality—not to violate them. But our young guard is mostly untrained in theatre-craft, even proud of his ignorance. He wishes to smash icons for the fun of it. To top it all is the government-inspired craze for folk forms. If you have not mastered your own craft, you cannot learn from another. Importing elements of folk drama into theatre when your grip on the theatre form itself is weak will create a hotch-potch that will finish you off as a director.

Similarly, bad acting seems to be a point of honour with many of our enthusiasts. They neglect the basic rules of speech and body-movement. They mumble, they slur, they are out of breath, they drop tails, they cannot come in on a cue. Any bit of dialogue which is not composed of their own extremely limited daily vocabulary leaves them gasping. They never recite poetry in their leisure hours. An actor who does not love poetry is a contradiction in terms. But since he knows he is deficient in recitative speech, uncertain of pronunciation and breathless to boot, he has recently taken to flaunting these weaknesses as his strengths, pretends that it is not necessary to learn to speak, that only old-fashioned actors spend a lifetime in fruitlessly practising the art of speaking, that mumbling and gasping are realistic modern acting. And if speech gets to be too damning a task, he will suddenly begin to throw his arms about in a burst of what is fancifully called physical acting. All these stunts are to get around the fact that many of our actors are incapable of coherent dialogue.

The one thing that our young enthusiasts could have learnt from the old professionals was how to speak. What we say at home and among friends is not what we are expected to say on the stage. The theatre is not an imitation of life, but its intensification in a focused form. Therefore, except in Mr Pinter's excessively dull plays, we are unlikely to find a string of 'How are you?', 'Wont you sit down?' and 'What are you drinking?' in the plays we are and shall be staging. A slice of life examined under the microscope yields the poetic speech of Lorca. It has to say much more than the daily rubbish because it has very little time. In theatre, speech becomes poetic to relate the speaker to life in general, to make the slice of life representative of the whole.

And no amount of physical acting, of arms sawing the air, will get our actor through dramatic speech, unless, like the American vandals we talked about earlier, we decide to cut speech out altogether from drama and replace it with groans and screams.

PSYCHOLOGY

At its height, bourgeois theatre produced psychological drama, Ibsen and Chekhov being the two giants who could keep their drawing-roomsful of bourgeoisie apparently calm and unperturbed while violent storms raged in their minds, culminating in sudden suicides and divorces. Both Ibsen and Chekhov pointed out, emphatically, that their plays indicated a way of life, the impasse into which the bourgeois families had led themselves (Chekhov's *Seagull* for instance). The endless leisure of the protagonists was very much like the forced leisure of the jobless in Gorky's *Lower Depths*. In that atmosphere of arrested activity the tragedy of Konstantin Treper gradually takes shape. Of course, the bourgeois milieu is constantly present before our eyes and is condemned implicitly in the play. But following Ibsen and Chekhov, a whole generation of playwrights has turned out a pretty impressive list of so-called psychological plays, where social causation is utterly and deliberately neglected, and the tragedy is generated by the hero's sex life, his hidden Oedipus complex and other badly digested and misunderstood theories of Freud. There are some very powerful writers among them—make no mistake about that.

Political theatre does not agree with this kind of obfuscation of the issue. You should not brand a person a psychopath and let all the action flow from that. If you do so, you are personalizing the problem, not socializing it. There can be no earthly reason to publicly show the case history of a lunatic. That is a violation of medical etiquette. Hamlet almost goes mad not because he sexually desires his mother but because his father has been killed by his uncle. That something is rotten in the state of Denmark and that things rank and gross in nature possess it are kept constantly in our view by Shakespeare.

But political theatre disagrees also with our playwrights who oversimplify the characters, who avoid psychological complexities. What we object to in the predominantly psychological play is not its portrayal of the violence of the human mind, but its exclusion of the social background. In our eagerness to portray a villainous capitalist and a working-class hero, we make both incredible—the one, a monster without a shred of human quality, and the other, a god without a shred of human weakness. Mao Zedong called these 'stick-and-straw puppets'. I too, let me confess, have often created such puppets in my plays. Marxian dialectics should help us understand that there is nothing absolutely white nor absolutely black in nature. And there is nothing that does not change. An immutable hero or villain is absurd.

But we understand why we make these mistakes—our prejudices and preferences colour our objectivity. Our hatred of the capitalist makes us exaggerate his evils; our love of the worker makes us overlook his personal faults. The Marxian definition of man is complex, and does not admit of oversimplification. Antonio Gramsci summarizes Marx thus:

> Man is a history of changing social relations. Each man is a whole history of relations—master and slave, lord and serf, capitalist and worker, king and subject, father and son, society and the individual, etc. And these relations are not static but constantly transforming themselves. Not only that. The moment man recognizes any of these relations, the relation changes; the act of recognition itself gives the relation a dimension that was not there before. For example the relation between the government and the individual. The moment the individual recognizes it for what it is, that it is class-coercion through the instrument of state, the relation can never be the same again; all the old ornamentation of loyalty, patriotism and duty falls away. The relation continues of course; otherwise the individual will go to jail. But now it is a qualitatively different relation; the individual accepts government only because he must, and looks upon it with disillusioned eyes. The relation between government and loyal individual has changed into one of government and disloyal individual.

The complexity of the Marxian conception of man should be a warning against creating straw puppets. As great a dramatist as Brecht withdrew in embarrassment from such a complex reading of man and declared that the definition was the ultimate in truth but could not be used for a play. Such complexity can never be captured in the portrait of a single man in a single play. So he decided not to try at all, and, instead, presented the various aspects of an individual in different scenes.

(Delivered as the Shriram Memorial Lectures, Shri Ram Center for Art and Culture, New Delhi, 13–15 January 1986.)

THEATRE AND IDEOLOGY

There is no reason to conceal the fact that this essay will rely entirely on a materialist theory of society, on a Marxist view of social forces. The problem of ideology is to give an account, within a materialist theory, of how social ideas arise. We need to understand what their role is in a particular social formation so as to inform the struggle to change society and open the road towards a socialist transformation of society. By 'ideology' we mean the mental framework—the languages, the concepts, the categories, the imagery of thought and the systems of representation—which the different classes deploy in order to define the way society works.

The work of the theatre is ideological—whether it consciously espouses the cause of a class or not, it must, willy-nilly, participate in the class struggle of ideas. Therefore it is vital for theatre to study the questions of how ideas come to grip the masses, dominate their social thinking and unite them from within. We must understand how ideas can reconcile a mass of people to a subordinate social place for great lengths of time, and how forms of consciousness arise and move that mass to action against the prevailing system.

At this moment, Marxism is being attacked by everyone—from sincere and profound thinkers to two-bit PR men from the state department. Everyone has some barbed remark about the changes, the turmoil in Eastern Europe. If we apply the method of Marxism to the troubles of the Communist parties of Eastern Europe—that new ideas ultimately spring from changes in the economic base—we shall be forced to concede that the technological revolution and the massive advance of the electronic media into the homes of the hitherto contented collective farmers have given rise to ideas of representative democracy which have in turn gripped the masses. It is significant that the problem is confined to Europe, and that the Communist parties of Asia and Africa are quite untouched by these convulsions.

The Tiananmen Square incident in Beijing is a case in point. The Indian media flooded us with stories of 5,000 students killed; the next morning it was 10,000 and the next, 15,000. While casualties snowballed, the American *Newsweek* magazine, unaware of the adventures of their Indian colleagues, reported 'a few scores' killed. The Indian newspapers changed track swiftly, and began to pursue Prime Minister Li Peng with all kinds of horror stories, including that he had been shot dead by a mutinous soldier. Then we heard he had been shot in the thigh. The next day, Beijing television showed Li Peng addressing the people's deputies with was no trace of a wound anywhere on his body. The press in India was concocting these stories to prove a turmoil in China which did not in reality exist. The Communists seemed to be comfortably in power and showed no inclination to dissolve their party or change its name.

An old Indian peasant, equally stoic and instinctively suspicious of anyone who hankers after worldly goods, when told of the demonstrations in Berlin and Bucharest, said to me, 'All they want is jeans.' Even if we put this down to the man's naivete, one cannot deny that the problems in Eastern Europe today are in a way problems of affluence. The Indian peasant may not appreciate the value of democratic rights, but he has been brought up in a stark tradition of self-denial and abnegation. All his saints have been hermits and fakirs. They have taught him for centuries that you go to meet your Maker naked, and only he who has not coveted wealth and luxury in this life can have happiness in the next. Therefore, all the talk of why productive forces in Eastern Europe are failing to fill shop-windows, or of East Germans desiring a better car than the Trabant, are banal and crudely mundane to him. The peasants in Asia and Africa, who cannot dream of possessing a car, find no logic in a section of humanity destroying the very basis of so many states for the sake of bodily comfort. You will forgive me if the examples in this essay are all culled from India. Being an Indian I could not do anything else.

Among the philosophical objections raised to the Marxist theory of ideology being the theoretical formulations of a class, the revisionist position often takes the form that Marx was wrong to imagine that particular ideas belong 'exclusively' to one particular class, as Laclau puts it (in *Politics and Ideology in Marxist Theory*, 1977), and that the very nature of language precludes the possibility of particular ideas being 'fixed permanently' to a class. Now this is imaginary Marxism. Far from claiming that particular ideas belong exclusively to a class, Marx repeatedly asserts that the ruling class infects other classes with its own ideas, so much so that the other classes imagine those ideas to be their own. Also, that no ideas are permanently fixed but are constantly in flux, even ultimately turning into their own opposites. Ideas may originate within a class but become socially relevant only by influencing other classes.

Other revisers, like Michel Foucault, end up abolishing the category 'ideology' altogether. More important is Louis Althusser's analysis of how ideology becomes internalized, and how other classes begin to imagine that it is necessary for their economic survival to embrace these ideas. We have seen these things happen before our eyes very recently. Practically the entire population of Germany, including its most civilized men, began to march and scream slogans of being a superior race. The ruling class wanted to whip the entire nation into a war, and its barbaric notions of racial superiority hid this naked class greed. Engels, in *Ludwig Feuerbach and the End of Classical German Philosophy* (1886), refers to the mediations which obscure the connection between ideas and economic base, especially in philosophy and religion. Even Stuart Hall, the Marxist, cannot help ridiculing the very notion of 'mediation'. But it is the mass of mediations which leads many critics to declare that they cannot see any connection between base and superstructure.

But if we take ancient India as an example and make even casual investigations into the much-vaunted philosophy of the Hindus and the Buddhists, we cannot help but notice the conscious efforts of the ruling classes to marshal religion to their own ends. Religious beliefs are a mere mask for class exploitation. The Buddhists used to recite *Dukhasangbedanaiba mayichaitanya-samahitang*, a daily prayer that says, 'Thou hast given me consciousness so that I may suffer.' Thus an entire nation became psychologically prepared to accept exploitation as God's dispensation, and the exploiter as God's agent. The more a man suffered in this birth, the greater his chances of better things in the next—the entire Hindu people became so imbued with this belief that even now the Indian villager looks upon self-flagellation as a means of attaining salvation from the cycle of births.

The entire religious code of the Hindus, based as it is on the division of society into four castes, seems to have been designed to keep the lowest caste, the shudra, the working man, in total subjection. Along with the shudra, the ruling classes also marked for special debasement various 'black' people, whom the scholar Haugh identifies as the original inhabitants of the country before the coming of the Indo-European tribes. The *Bajsaneyi Samhita* stipulates that, during the Purushmedh Yagna, a chandal, an aboriginal, must be sacrificed. The *Aitereya Brahman* records that a shudra may be physically beaten whenever the upper castes choose. The shudra's right to learning was taken away; a shudra caught reciting the Vedas would be promptly put to death. In the *Shranta Sutra*, the shudra has only the right to wash the feet of upper-caste students.

Scholars who have studied the masses of self-contradictory religious edicts of the Vedic age have come to the conclusion that between BC 1000 and 500, shudra workers, such as blacksmiths, chariot-makers and peasants, adopted the non-Aryan god Shiva as their object of worship and thus attempted to escape the rigours of the Hindu caste structure. The result was a further hardening of the code and stipulation of heavier penalties for transgressing it.

The older book of Jaimini declared land to be common property and therefore not to be divided among sons; in fact, it could not be gifted. Hereafter, we begin to come across large land-holdings where shudras worked as hired labour. This was the time when Gautama, in his *Apastamba Sutra,* clearly stated that the task of the shudra was to serve the three upper classes; his way to salvation lay through obedient labour. One reads in the Gita the celebrated line, 'You have no right except to work. The fruit of it does not concern you.' We have had volumes of commentaries on the philosophical implications of this saying of the Lord Krishna but hardly anyone dwells on its primary, literal meaning—that workmen should only work and that the fruit belongs to someone else. The hidden philosophical meanings may all be very well, but one cannot altogether ignore the apparent one either.

Our interpretation is reinforced by the religious laws of the time, where the *Vinayapitaka* defines a workman as *ahatak*—one who can be whipped. The *Apastamba* lays down that a peasant who resigns from work is to be physically tortured. Gautama has an interesting clause: an Aryan of higher caste, though never socially meeting a shudra, may, in case he is marrying his daughter or spending money on a religious ceremony, extort money from shudras by fair means or foul. Jacobi, in the series *Sacred Books of the East* (Max Müeller ed., 1879–1910), gives us a translation of the Pali text *Swagadam* which appears to have been written by people who took sadistic delight in even recounting acts of torture. Listing punishments for disobedient workmen, the passage recommends imprisonment in an iron cage, breaking the legs, cutting off the lips, boring a hole in the foot, tearing the tongue out, tying the guilty to the tail of a mad bull, burning at the stake and so on, until death.

The great law-giver Manu can be seen during this same time to be devising religious taboos and rules to force people to work; he declares that a king who fails to keep the four castes strictly divided is destroyed along with his kingdom. He makes a comment that suddenly reveals the essential weakness of the state based on forced labour: that a kingdom should be founded in areas where the Aryans are in a majority; if a kingdom is built on a land where shudras are more numerous (*shudrabhuyistha*), it will soon be destroyed.

The *Vayu Purana* records the legend of Pramiti who collected a band of armed brahmans to go around slaughtering shudras and raiding their villages. Manu also issues a virtual call to arms:

Shastrang dwijatibhir—grahyang dharma yatroparudhyate
Dwijatinang cha varnanang biplabe kalkarite.

Historians agree that this was the period when the Kushan, Saka and Greek kings on the north-western borders of India began to send raiding parties into the country. Since these foreigners were hated by the arrogant Aryans, the shudras appeared to have made common cause with the invaders and, in large tracts of northern India, rose against the three upper castes. Hence, religion now turned militant and advocated the slaughter of its own, most numerous caste. Correspondence between religion and class interest here is naked and without mediation, in spite of every law beginning with an invocation to the all-seeing and all-forgiving Brahma.

This hatred of working men, rising from relations of production, permeated every aspect of ancient Indian ideology, in poetry, literature and theatre. Bharata's *Natyashastra*, formulating the laws of drama, raised a censorious voice against making a shudra the hero of a play. No other culture has been so insistent on noble birth as a precondition for important characters in drama, and it took a brave playwright to write a play like *Mrichhakatika* (The Little Clay Cart by Shudraka) where thieves, drunks and gamblers indulge horseplay—a refreshing change. The *Natyashastra* allowed low-born characters on stage such as guards, courtesans and crowds. But they were not allowed to profane Sanskrit by speaking it. Sanskrit could be spoken only by the gods, and Aryan riff-raff and women spoke a Prakrit dialect on stage. Nay, more—the *Natyashastra* banned the writing of tragedy, lest it offend the artistic sensibility of the higher caste audience. While all plays were supposed to end happily, the *Natyashastra* explored all possibilities in the use of the hands and body, the tone and volume of voice projection. It is obvious that only a connoisseur could follow an old Indian play in full. This was only natural because the masses were strictly barred from the theatre.

Marxism demands we look at every phenomenon historically. Thus, we need to look at the Indian workman against a long tradition of the deprivation of his rights. The religion preached for centuries makes him believe that he is born to suffer; anything else will somehow be a sin. But ancient Indian philosophy had its atheist side too—it denies the possibility of God and is grounded in materialism. Such was the Charvaka philosophy, the dialectics of Jaimini and Buddhist atheist thought. But Hindu religion, law, mythology and epic soon went after them with slander and abuse; in the Indian mind, Charvaka transformed into a cannibal (*rakshas*). So effective and vast was the propaganda that the Indian villager considers himself polluted if he so much as thinks of the name of Charvaka. In the Mahabharata, Charvaka has been irrelevantly dragged in as a friend of the wicked king Duryodhana, suggesting that all the evil schemes that the king devises have been suggested by this demonic friend.

Thus when the other theatre, the theatre of ideas, the theatre of revolt, tries to now speak to the Indian workmen, it faces not just an exploited class but a concept of life; it faces 3,000 years of resignation and surrender. These, together with class relations, constitute a worker.

The pseudo-Marxists keep postulating that since the production relation condemns the worker to creating surplus value, the mere act of explaining it to him will wake him from his stupor. But this has been repeatedly proved as an oversimplification and, therefore, false. In India, the problem is not, as Stuart Hall puts it, the worker's desire for his 'pay-packet' (Mr Hall's insistence on the 'pay-packet' itself appears to be an offshoot of advanced capitalism). Rather, it is that the religious propaganda of the ruling classes has succeeded so well that the worker thinks it is his own idea; it has become second nature to him. Psychologists need to analyse the nature of this thralldom.

When challenged, this vague feeling perhaps feeds on the race-memory of oppression and torture, and the worker becomes aggressively stubborn.

As we have seen, certain critics of Marxism assume that Marx was in favour of fixing a particular idea to a particular class. Marx, of course, never said anything of the sort; he discerned that within a class are various blocs, each with radically different ideas of social forces. They are all united because they all want their class to dominate, but, often, the unity dissolves and the blocs come out fighting one another. The whole of the *Eighteenth Brumaire* is a study of different ideas germinating within one ruling class—the ideas of the Bourbon monarchists, bankers, financiers, petty bourgeois, aristocracy, adventurers around Louis Bonaparte. Far from fixing any one idea to a class, Marx was grappling with conflicting ideas while struggling against the ideas of the working class. Within the working class too, one can assume, a multiplicity of ideas and struggles for ascendancy. Among the Indian workers also, a bloc will advance rapidly and another will be frightened of ghosts. The workmen in one part of the country will conquer even religious dictation and, in another, prostrate themselves before clay images of gods.

The Indian ruling class is not a homogeneous bloc but an alliance of several classes which pull the government this way and that. The advanced bourgeois, who believes in industrial power, has to work closely with the superstitious moneylender. The landlord, who holds vast tracts of land and extorts rent, is a partner of the ruling bloc. Not only is such a conglomeration unable to maintain consistency, it also contradicts itself at every point. This would be sufficient for some critics to claim that Marx's postulation about the basis determining ideas had been disproved. On the contrary, it further strengthens Marx's theory, that each class and bloc rests on a different set of production relations and that their interests often clash. The industrial bourgeois would like very much to solve the agrarian question once and for all, so that the peasants, over 70 per cent of the country's population, have purchasing power and thus form a huge domestic market for industrial goods. The landlord who shares power with the bourgeois will have none of it, because he wants to preserve the rural economy. The contradiction between the two viewpoints is total, and this is reflected in almost all the policies the government formulates.

The ideological superstructure is thus confusing and reflective of various trends and sub-trends. On the one hand, the ideology of the ruling classes is one unending eulogy of the bliss of machinery. Nehru once addressed the steel factories as 'the new temples of worship'. On the other hand, we are treated to numerous literary works and films that curse machines and city life as the twin disasters which have destroyed the supposed peace of forest life. We see direct government propaganda for science, along with equally visible propaganda (which the government passively accepts) for the most dastardly superstitions and miracles. On the one hand, we have numerous government committees on women's freedom, and, on the other, a far greater number of films, novels and TV serials which proceed to prove that it is peculiarly Indian for a woman to grovel at her husband's feet. For years since 1947, the Congress government and Party indulged in colourful rhetoric on how women will have to be free. Then it brought a Bill in Parliament and had it passed by brute majority that a Muslim who divorces his wife need not pay alimony. It has always been a part of this party's ideological offensive to claim that it has built the world's largest democracy. It proclaimed an Emergency in the country for two years, censoring all newspapers and sending the entire Opposition to jail without trial, repeating all the while that India was the world's largest democracy.

This party which talks of building democracy hates democracy itself and has not held elections for 15 years. It clings to the creed of 'one leader, one party, one country' in a manner that is reminiscent of the Nazis. Mrs Indira Gandhi, its leader, was almost canonized in her lifetime by faithful writers and artists. A leading painter of India conceived her as Goddess Durga—riding a lion and slaying the monster. Her assassination by her own guards who happened to be Sikhs immediately sparked a gruesome massacre of Sikh men, women and children in Delhi, with the army looking on.

Mr Rajiv Gandhi, her son, when asked why such outrages were taking place, shrugged and said, 'When a big tree falls, the earth trembles.' The Congress(I) rushed through this man's election to his mother's post, helped by the TV which, for weeks, kept flashing pictures of Mrs Gandhi's burning body and a desolate Rajiv howling at her feet. Then his own government appointed a commission to inquire into the murder of Mrs Gandhi although its report was swiftly suppressed. The press, however, managed to learn that no Sikh was involved in the conspiracy; it was led by one R. K. Dhawan whom Mr Rajiv Gandhi had promoted to the post of chief political adviser after coming to know of the commission's findings. When a big tree falls, the earth trembles—the earth began to tremble with rumblings of suspicion and questions. If Mr Gandhi's own adviser plotted Mrs Gandhi's assassination, why did gangs of Congress(I) hoodlums, defiantly waving their party flag, attack Sikhs in Delhi? Why was the inquiry commission's report suppressed by Mr Gandhi? Finally, Mr Gandhi got thoroughly embroiled in the Bofors bribery case and was thrown, by popular vote, out of power.

The uneven development of the various parts of India is dramatically highlighted by the fact that in one state, West Bengal, the Communists are leading a Left Front government for the last 12 years.

This fact too has its roots in the cultural history of Bengal—the state where an extremely strong movement against religious bigotry and superstition has raged since the 1820s, and where Rammohun Roy, Henry Louis Vivian Derozio, Iswarchandra Vidyasagar and Swami Vivekananda are household names. Naturally, the ideological struggle against the ossified religious traditions of India was bound to be more intense in this part of the country.

The Congress(I) government has ruled India almost uninterruptedly for 43 years. During this time, not only has the ideology of the ruling classes permeated every art form in India but the government has also tried to forcibly suppress such expressions of working-class ideology as it considered particularly dangerous—for example, the people's theatre movement, which takes the theatre of revolt to working-class slums and peasant areas. In 1876, the British government promulgated an ordinance which gave the police the power to censor plays, either to excise parts of them or ban them altogether. Scores of plays were thus banned and playscripts burnt publicly. It even became an issue in the freedom struggle. But when the Congress managed to scramble to the seat of power in 1947, it did not annul the 1876 Ordinance; on the contrary, it used it more vigorously than the English and banned any play that spoke of resistance to the ruling classes—bourgeois, landlord or moneylender. Even classics did not escape their attention. In West Bengal, only when the Communist Party came to power with its Leftist allies was the 1876 Act finally buried. But that did not end the problem. The Congress militants were not to be put off by so slight a thing as the law; they began attacking theatre groups and audiences with bombs and guns, thus breaking up performances.

The ruling classes may have various differences with one another in their approach to the economic question, but on one major ideological point they are more or less united: they all wish to make effective use of religion to keep the working classes divided. Some do it aggressively, calling for a Hindu empire where Muslims, Sikhs and Christians will have no place. Others, like the Congress(I), mouth endless platitudes about secular democracy but, in action, often organize pogroms against the minorities, as was already evident during the anti-Sikh riots.

The moment Mr Rajiv Gandhi felt that the people of India were about to reject his party, he too realized the need to go one better than the militant Hindu fascists. We began to see him in temples with a red dot on his forehead, prostrating himself before all kinds of medieval gods and goddesses. Finally he and his home minister, Buta Singh (not a Hindu either), visited the hermit Deoraha Baba who lives atop a *machan* and bestows his blessing upon the devotees below with a sharp kick to the head. For weeks, the TV showed the two ministers smiling beatifically while being thus kicked.

Mr Gandhi and the ruling clique decided to fish deeper in religious waters when they got themselves thoroughly involved in the Babri Masjid controversy. This was a mosque built by Emperor Babar where Muslims prayed regularly. Some Hindu fanatics suddenly decided that it was built on the precise spot marking the birthplace of Ram, the mythical king believed by some Hindus to have been God incarnate. Of course, history doubts if Ram ever lived at all. But Mr Gandhi's encouragement drove Hindu fanatics to declare that they would demolish the mosque and build a temple to Ram at the same spot. For this, bricks inscribed with the name of Ram were worshipped all over India and sent by trucks to the site. Thus a new god appeared in the Hindu pantheon—the common brick—and processions bearing the bricks made their way through areas where Muslims lived, leading to clashes, the one at Bhagalpur in Bihar being the bloodiest. Corpses are still being discovered in paddy-fields and wells, mostly of women and children. Mr Gandhi himself opened his election campaign with a speech at Ayodhya where Ram's temple is proposed to be built. He invoked the aid of Ram in the coming battle of the ballot, and his Hindu audience replied with aggressive religious slogans.

At the session of the History Congress soon to follow, a yellow robed holy man forced his way to the stage with the help of armed hooligans and harangued the historians on the historicity of Ram and his kingdom without any signs of police intervention. Thus was official patronage offered to the peddlers of the slogan, 'Down with science and knowledge' and 'Up with myth and superstition'.

The TV, meanwhile, totally state-owned in India, did its bit in deepening this ideology of darkness. For years, every Sunday morning, it telecast the Ramayana, especially emphasizing Ram's divinity and miraculous powers—men sailing across the sky without any mechanical aid. The Ramayana, however, portrays every non-Aryan tribe that Ram comes across on his journey south as monkeys or cannibals. The TV Ramayana preserved that aspect and we were presented with the spectacle of talking monkeys and bears. The serial thus not only made absurdities real, but also preached a trend of racial hatred that would put the Nazi *Herrenvolk* to shame. One would imagine that such asinine propaganda would be laughed away by the masses. But that was not the case—these religious beliefs are too deeply ingrained in the minds of the Indian working men. The TV Ramayana struck a chord in their hearts that is frightening to contemplate. On Sunday mornings, India stopped working; the roads were deserted for everyone was home, watching the exploits of the god-king. When the Ramayana ended, the Mahabharata began. Now it was all war for the purity of India, an appeal to take up arms to return India to her pristine Hindu glory. If one watched closely, one realized that the entire programme was a noisy sabre-rattling appeal to blood-lust.

The film industry in India, totally dominated by big business, plays up the young hero as the saviour of the masses; his fists fly at the sinners and put all evils to right, much as Ram the god-king solves the problems of his kidnapped wife. This hero sometimes appears as a poor man, even a working man, but, towards the end of the film, we are told he is not really a plebian but the lost son of a millionaire. Three thousand years after Manu wrote his laws, a shudra is still not permitted to be the hero. What one never sees either is poor men organizing collective resistance—the single crusader is all one is allowed. Also, the films unearth every forgotten cult from the dung-heap of some unknown village deep in the heart of India.

As for theatre: the governmental machinery is geared to forcing all theatre groups to adopt idioms of folk theatre, whether such idioms help the play or not. To pick at random a bit of folk theatre from here and there ruins the folk as well as the theatre. There is one group for example, which has discovered big drums and gymnastics somewhere in central India, and all its plays, irrespective of content, look the same—everybody is constantly somersaulting on stage while big drums shake the house. The result of all this is the destruction of the importance of content and the glorification of form for form's sake. This same group proposed to do a play on a village marriage and Shakespeare's *Hamlet* in the same form. This just goes to show that, for such exponents of theatre, the form is the thing—it is too important to change, even for the sake of Shakespeare.

We have already referred to the theatre of revolt which, in spite of direct raids by police and gangsters, continues to uphold the supremacy of ideas over form. Behind it is the ideology of another class which itself suffers from contradictions, illusions and rank backwardness. The theatre of revolt also suffers from these limitations. It has, in the past, tried to conquer these by narrow insistence on ideology and on a convenient mouthing of Marxist terminology. But the realization has dawned, I think, that theatre is addressed to a working class that is steeped in rotten tradition. To fight the ideology of the ruling classes, the world's theatre and literature must steep itself in the knowledge of exactly what makes the working man the willing tool of his exploiters.

(Read at the International Theatre Seminar, University of Lancaster, 5–9 April 1990. Published in two consecutive issues of *The Saturday Statesman*, June 1990.)

Innovation and Experimentation in Theatre

A question I would like to revisit is one that has been raised repeatedly since Jean-Paul Sartre declared that he did not believe literature made any impression on people: does drama affect the people at all? Does theatre make any impression on society? Or has it been a dreadful waste of time these past 5,000 years? Does the theatre of ideas result in a single convert at the end of the performance? Why has mankind expended so much labour, time and talent in order to shepherd a few hundred people into an unhygienically stuffy room in which they then remain confined for three to four hours, watching a make-believe game of pretend emotions?

There has to be a sound sociological reason for such phenomenon and in that reason lies the social utility of the theatre. Psychologists who have studied theatre audiences agree that the very act of sitting close together and watching a tragedy unifies the spectators, makes them more sympathetic to one another, makes of so many different individuals a body of kinsmen. Psychologists call this 'affiliation under stress'—a group of individuals sharing the same danger and stress tend to draw closer to one another. From this arises battle-line comradeship in war, and the lifelong friendships that began in the bomb-shelters of London during the Blitz. In the theatre, the danger is simulated, but, if the theme of the play is such that it resonates with the audience's life and if the characters are so drawn from reality that the audience recognizes or identifies with them, the effect on the audience is almost as if it has been threatened with a real danger during the performance. The result is affiliation, unification. Human beings, from the time they became civilized, have used theatre to foster unity among themselves; theatre, thus, contributed to the formation of the political self.

At the same time, the 'theory of affiliation under stress' is a strong argument against those who still seek to keep drama and theatre away from social reality. A theatre that merely entertains and avoids any reference to real social or political problems will never be able to subject the audience to stress; hence, such an audience will not affiliate. Such a theatre denies the very reason of theatre's creation. A theatre that stages the classics of Shakespeare and Sophocles must remember how modern Shakespeare and Sophocles were, and that their plays depict such universal human emotions that a contemporary Indian audience can identify with them as easily as if they had been written in this country and for this age.

On the other hand, we watched with consternation the way in which the Indian state decided to present India's greatest classics, the Ramayana and the Mahabharata, on TV, bringing to a head the conflict between tradition and experiment. How is tradition able to inspire new worlds in theatre? Well, Indian TV solved it very simply: it left it to the big capitalist boys to decide the question. Thus we had epics in the service of soap and shampoo manufacturers, mindless glitz, golden costumes, thunderous laughter from all kinds of villains, arrows exploding like scud missiles, cardboard chariots painted in the colours of the rainbow, monkeys and bears speaking Sanskritized Hindi, holy men flying over painted clouds—in short, a fairytale written by an alcoholic. Totally lost in all this confusion is the tragedy of the girl Sita, the man and lover Ram, the vacillation of the soldier Arjuna who does not want to fight his kinsmen. Bloodthirsty howls are all that the makers have found worth preserving from two of the greatest books mankind has created. There is not a moment of human passion or cowardice, weakness, pity, mercy, love or forgiveness in these commercialized serials. And since there is no humanness, the question of audience identification or stress never arises for even a moment. Everyone is enjoying a good old wives' tale and to hell with the classics.

The Indian capitalist is notorious for his philistinism, for a kind of illiterate vulgarity towards the art, and he tries to foist this concept of drama on the entire country. The TV is his principal weapon and it has been surrendered to the whims of the so-called sponsors. Everything has to be sponsored by a soap-maker, whether it is a film by Satyajit Ray or a concert by Ravi Shankar. Unless it carries the presumptuous announcement right in the middle of the show, 'This part of the programme was sponsored by Messers Idiot and Fool, makers of Shoe-Polish', it cannot be telecast. This is just an indication of the gradual hegemony that the capitalist is extending over the entire cultural world. He wants Indian music, Indian theatre and Indian cinema to reflect his own taste and personality. His tastes, proverbially flippant, are shaped by film magazines. He has neither the time nor the education to probe any deeper. But deep within him is an unscrupulous urge for absolute power which has surfaced significantly in the two epic serials. In the final analysis, both were thoughtless, unreasoning glorifications of an imaginary past, attempts to rouse blind jingoistic pride with clear undertones of racism, unmistakable incitements to bloodshed and extermination, and forays into sanctifying the code of a primitive tribal war in modern times. Then, when riots broke out in Ayodhya and other places, the state pretended surprise and innocence. The state itself had, for a period of over two years, carried out the bourgeois's design of throwing the country into turmoil so that they could install even more sycophantic stooges in power. The two TV serials were a foretaste of what Indian fascism could do to the arts if it ever storms into power.

Thus, when we talk of the tradition in theatre, we must not only think of form and what the folk theatre has preserved for us in the matter of direct uninterrupted appeals to a mass audience, the dynamism of the arena or the use of songs and dances—all that is very interesting, no doubt, but we must also consider the question of the *content* of traditional themes. The Ramayana and the Mahabharata have traditionally provided our playwrights with numerous themes for modern plays. Now, with the vulgarized TV serials, a serious problem has arisen. The audience asks: why does not your costume glitter? Why does not your Duryodhana laugh? Why are there no chariots and battles? Why does your Krishna talk so much in the boring scene before the battle? This is, of course, the scene where Krishna expounds the Gita, contemptuously curtailed in the TV serial in order to quickly get back to the action. Cheap things have a remarkable capacity for nullifying the effect of any artistic creation. A publisher in East Berlin recently made a sad confession: for the last 45 years, Tolstoy had been at the top of his sales list, but, with the unification of Germany and the cancellation of subsidies to serious bookshops, Frederick Forsyth has taken over and Tolstoy struggles to be remembered. Great art cannot just be left to the freedom of what the Americans call market economy—it has to be protected and carefully propagated among the masses—just as the law can never say that drugs and narcotics should be left to the mercy of profiteers who will inevitably corrupt and debase the people's taste by brisk trading in trash.

On the other hand, even the most serious theatre-worker in this country appears to face a problem of form: he is now haunted by the ghost of folk forms. The state connives by offering cash aid to anyone who uses anything that sounds or looks folkish. Our theatre-workers, hard-pressed for cash, immediately embark on a form-finding tour to the nearest countryside and pick up a song or two, or half a dance, and hasten back to the city to toss their discovery hugger-mugger into whatever play they have been planning. The result does credit neither to folk art nor to the art of the theatre nor to the intelligence of such enthusiasts. It is my humble opinion that experiments in theatre can certainly draw from folk forms, as from many other sources, but not in this slapdash manner. A lifetime's work is required to master the elements of a folk form to sufficiently mould them for use in theatre. A couple of dances, or a chorus in exotic costume, does not constitute experiment in theatre form, and they ruin the play as well.

Then, of course, there is the question of worshipping form to the neglect of content, as is apparent in the work of some theatre groups in the country. One of them is so enamoured of what they allege to be an authentic folk form in central India that they pour every play, like molten lead, into the mould of the same form. This form relies on big drums and robust dancing—ideally suited for the outdoors where it was born, but, in the close confines of a modern auditorium, it is too loud for the senses. And when one hears that this group has produced Shakespeare's *Hamlet* and subjected it to the same nerve-wracking treatment, one is simply horrified. Form in the theatre is handmaiden to content; each play must find its own form, and the director must begin a fresh search for form every time he handles a new play. To set up a single rigid form into which every play must be fitted is either his unpardonable pride or his unpardonable laziness.

Also, experiment cannot mean a cavalier rejection of tradition—a new theatre cannot be born out of thin air. I have noticed this trend in parts of the Calcutta theatre world, as you must have come across it in other parts of India. It involves a gangster's way of looking at life, at society, at parents, at literature, at everything people hold in reverence, and it is an attitude intimately connected to the same celebrated market economy. To the cynical producers of this market, nothing is sacred in the culture of this country or of any other, for that matter. To such terribly disgruntled young men, there has never been a dramatist in this country, nor has there ever been anything that may be styled as theatre. They find Shakespeare unintelligible and dull, and therefore adapt every modern European crime-thriller or rotten farce into an Indian language and perform it in the confidence that it will be the foundation of the hitherto non-existent Indian theatre.Then when people fail to turn up at the box-office, they blame their backwardness and ignorance.

An experiment that denies its own past is bound to be still-born; Bertolt Brecht used to say that an experiment means understanding tradition and then bringing it forward to our age. He studied theatre forms and the technique of playwriting from all parts of the world and from all ages, even Chinese opera, in order to evolve new ones. It is a false belief that he hit upon something called 'epic theatre' and then used it on all occasions. Brecht, in fact, used different techniques for different plays. (His production of *Señora Carrar's Rifles* (1937), for example, was thoroughly Stanislavskian.) Even his 'epic theatre' cannot be said to be one unfailing formula for every kind of drama. It was, rather, a name given to a style of looking at reality and did not signify rigidity of production technique. Brecht's productions of *Days of the Commune* (1956) and *The Resistible Rise of Arturo Ui* (1958) are as different from each other as if two different *régisseurs* had conceived them.

Experimentation thus begins from the technique of playwriting itself, from the way the dramatist looks at life and society. Certain conventions inevitably develop to which dramatists repeatedly take resort (because they are said to be successful devices for winning applause) until the conventions become a dead habit without any relevance to real human emotions or real social situations. Therefore, experimentation must begin at the very beginning and must be a new outlook on life which will faithfully capture the contradictions of present-day social life, the complexities of character-development that must inevitably result and a special complication of plot that will not merely repeat the convention of theatrical intensity but will adequately reflect as it is today.

When one studies the evolution of Brecht's technique of writing—his analytical study of characters, his presentation of several alternative ends to the same play, his frequent device of splitting a character into two or more alter-persona—one can feel the entire history of European drama behind it. One can see traces of the morality play—good and evil struggling for the soul of man, one can feel the impact of man. One can feel the impact of Goethe's *Faust*, especially if we agree with Jung's study of Faust: Jung regards Faust's personality as alienated from him in a kind of *dementia praceox*, so that when Faust talks to Mephistopheles he is, in reality, talking to himself. That is Goethe's experiment with Shakespearean soliloquy. If Brecht is the greatest experimenter in the theatre of this century it is because his experiments were not rootless and contemptuous of the heritage of world theatre. This in turn was due to his Marxist view of life which helped give old idioms of theatre a new lease of life.

One last question needs to be raised here: why must the theatre constantly experiment? Why can't it drift along paths already charted and used by others? There is, of course, the problem of life and society changing constantly; an experiment today becomes a cliché tomorrow, so banal and commonplace that its intrusion in the play repels the audience. We return to the point we tried to make at the outset, regarding the function of drama—to unify the audience under stress. If a worn-out cliché masquerading as experiment intrudes in a performance, the spectator is, at that moment, freed from stress because he is forcibly reminded that he is in a theatre and that the events on stage are false and cannot possibly happen to him. Immediately, the theatre denies its function in society.

This is especially true in the era of the much eulogized market economy—capitalism, in short. A theatre practitioner will tell you how it is becoming more and more difficult to reach an audience and hold its attention. This is inevitable—in this society, profiteering is the great virtue and money is religion. People are alienated from all their own faculties, except the faculty of possession. They are alienated from their language, their sentiments of pity, love, sympathy and respect; the sole desire to possess takes the place of all. To reach the mind of such an audience, the *régisseur* must use experiments in form in the manner of a weapon—to shock, startle, shake or persuade. Unfamiliar and challenging plays would rouse such an alienated audience, make them sit up and take notice.

The destruction caused by capitalism in the field of culture is almost as if vandals have ridden over it. Our young theatre-workers go out in naive enthusiasm to find folk theatre in the villages; what they do not realize is that which they are discovering and gathering in their loving arms are the distorted bits and pieces of an art shattered by profiteers. I can speak from my experience of Jatra in Bengal, with which I worked professionally for 10 years. Every aspect of Jatra is now commercially urged, commercially oriented and commercially prostituted. Hardly anything of the vigorous indigenous folk theatre survives.

But Jatra still has one great advantage over us—it is much closer to the masses, and reacts immediately to their needs and demands. By going through the repertoire of the 60-odd professional Jatra troupes in Bengal every year, you can tell pretty accurately what the rural masses are thinking. This is no mean achievement. Granted these plays are done for profit alone, but, in this society, profit is the only criterion of popularity, and a Jatra play has to respond to a need in the people in order to make money. A clever statistician can—by preserving his distance and without being swayed by Jatra's boast of purity and pristine passion—simply by calculating the sale figures and the types of plays, have a clear idea of the political and social currents presently flowing in Bengal.

As I was saying, Jatra experiments in production are commercial in character. They are merely gimmicks, wholly lacking artistic merit. But where Jatra experiments command attention are in the field of play writing. The promptness with which playwrights try to capitalize on current issues and work out theatrical devices to make their point provide interesting material. For example, since the American aggression against Iraq, as many as six Jatra plays have been written, rehearsed and are now being played all over the countryside; all of them feature Saddam Hussain as the leader of a great anti-imperialist war. I have not seen any, but have talked to the writer-director of one of such play. He says, 'If Iraq loses, it will be India's turn next.' His play opens with Mr Bush being handed the Nobel Peace Prize. The citation, read out by a sycophantic representative of the Western countries declares, 'President Bush, this prize for Peace goes to you for waging war and for kicking arse as you promised. We note with satisfaction that the Iraqi soldiers who deprived Kuwait of her freedom have been annihilated in Baghdad by precision bombing, especially those among them who are now between six months and nine months old.' I am told this brings the house to its feet every time, laughing, cheering and shouting anti-war slogans.

Of course, nothing has transpired in the Jatra world to compete with Jabbar Patel's brilliant use of Natyasangeet in his production of Vijay Tendulkar's *Ghashiram Kotwal*, or come within miles of the experiments of Girish Ghosh from 1872 to the first decade of this century when he tried to synthesize classical European theatre with Jatra. All the same, the intimacy of Jatra with its audience, their interaction, may lead in the near future to the development of a theatrical experiment that will capture the global reality for the Indian people more eloquently.

(Read at the National Seminar on Indian Literature: An End-Century Assessment. Organized by Sahitya Akademi at the India International Centre, New Delhi, 20–24 February 1991.)

OVERVIEWS / REVIEWS / REPORTS / COMMENTS

Shakespeare and the Modern Stage

The day, when a vague eulogy of Shakespeare was permissible, is long past. Shakespeare's literary supremacy is apparent to anyone who appreciates literature as a law of nature. But that he symbolizes the potency of the human intellect does not always denote, to his admirers, his achievements in the outer world. There is in his work the constant process of values being reasserted, of a number of values being acclaimed as absolute.

Othello begins with the premise that all human beings are to be trusted and Othello expects from all mankind the nobility that he himself never fails to give. His faith in man is tested through a series of dramatic scenes—by the moral nihilism of Iago, by the Oriental emotionalism of his own Moorish blood and by other forces of the peculiar medieval social system. We see his ethics being shaken, the absolute values subverted and, soon, the loss of all faith in men and women. And his noble nature feels no remorse, even at murder. But the trial is soon over and Shakespeare firmly re-establishes the absolute values as unquestionable by making Othello destroy himself. There is, similarly, the quality of mercy in *The Merchant of Venice*. And *Macbeth,* which ultimately establishes conscience. And so it happens, for every serious work undertaken by Shakespeare. These values, being absolute, are eternal. Therefore they are absolute today.

A modern interpretation of Shakespeare must typify his place, not in the past but in the present life of the nation and the world. It ought to constitute a perpetual reminder of the position that he fills in the present economy, and is likely to fill in the future economy of human thought. A reminder for those whose growing absorption in the narrowing business of life tends to make them forget it and take Shakespeare merely as a hypocritical satisfaction of their aesthetic consciences.

Much of the conventional theatrics associated with Shakespeare must therefore go—the extravagant grease-paint, the yelling mouth and the gaudy satin. Since people all over the world are reconsidering conscience, the objectives and the habits of enormous human masses, it is the business of the artistes to stand at the forefront of this process. No one can be independent of this collective responsibility and shun the realism of the age, and no one, therefore, can quote the supposed sanctity of Shakespeare.

The principal media at the disposal of the theatre are decor, acting and direction. For 300 years, these media have conveyed Shakespeare on the basis of a sanctified theory. This theory, we have seen, is obsolete. The media, therefore, must develop on new lines and these lines must be defined.

What has consistently been forgotten during these 300 years is the responsibility of each medium to the production as a whole. Whereas the dramatist establishes a direct link between theatre and life, the producer strives to achieve unity within the production with the aid of sundry forms of stage expression at his disposal. An identical task confronts the designer and the actor, who, at par with the director, should be responsible for the production as a whole.

But what actually happened?

The scenic designer tried to earn immortality by mounting on stage an elaborate canvas and a riot of colour, hoping the audience would ignore the actors and the story and acclaim him a Titan instead. The actors devoted their energies to being as prominent as possible. The producer, in his turn, disagreed, and interpolated tableaux, masques and pageants to attract the audience to what he thought was otherwise a dull experience. Thus the most collective of all arts, the art of the stage, became a battlefield. This essentially wrong approach persists. The result: the disintegration of the wonderful texture of Shakespeare into discordant components—into the neurotic actor, the militant decor-artist and directorial slapstick.

Let us take the decor first. Charles Kean and his school, who first set the example of lavish designs, paid for their excesses by running into disastrous financial losses. Why? In comedies dealing with the ridiculous aspects of modern sophisticated society and in tragedies revealing the horrible spectacles of the contemporary social conflicts, the stage presentation definitely relies to a great extent on the realism of scenic appliances. The Dublin Street scene in Sean O'Casey's *Red Roses for Me* (1943) and the Old Vic production of *An Inspector Calls* (1946) strike us to the core because, to a large degree, the settings are so true to life. But that is not the case with Shakespeare. The organic unity of his works lies in his system of universal values. These values appeal to the highest faculties of thought and imagination, and the pursuit of realism in Shakespearean scenery tends to destroy the significance of the illusion which it ought instead to enforce.

Complex and obtrusive stage machinery exaggerates for the spectator the inevitable gap between the visionary and indeterminate limits of the scene as imagined by the poet, and the cramped and narrow version which the stage renders practicable. All that is to be attempted and desired in Shakespearean production is effective suggestion. Whereas Herbert Tree got scores of carpenters and builders to set up a barrage of hammer-thudding between every two acts and secured only a mimicry of Prospero's island (and overshadowed the actors), a modern producer can convey exactly the mysterious weirdness with a white pin-spot relieving the lines on the actor's face on an otherwise dark stage. Therefore the scenic designer for the modern Shakespeare should not inspire his decor with an independent life of its own but bring out, in each separate scene and in the whole set, the kernel of the play, the spirit of the action and the characters. And this should make him subdue himself in one case while giving full scope to the artistic support of the cast in the other.

In England, in 1844, Samuel Phelps first launched this movement for simplicity. Apart from the artistic gain from adjusting decor to its relevant position, such a revolution saved an enormous amount of money which Phelps used in other ways, especially raising the standard of acting by trebling the pay of the cast. It needs little logic to see that this economy lessens the financial risk involved in a Shakespearean production, and raises the morale. Scientific simplification has become a theory now; Nugent Monk produced *King Lear* at Maddermarket Theatre, Norwich, with a throne set on an old Anglo-Saxon stone structure; the rest was left to curtains and light. Little Theatre, always at the forefront of the British progressive dramatic movement, put across *Julius Caesar* in modern costume, no doubt relying on the one sentence of Cassius after the murder of Caesar:

How many ages hence

> Shall this lofty scene be acted over,
> In states unborn and accents yet unknown.
>
> (Act III, scene 1)

And Fascist Italy had already been born to make the historical parallel necessary to justify taking Cassius at his word. Laurence Olivier's cinematic adaptation of *Hamlet* is a masterpiece in restricting setting to the bare stoniness of Elsinore Castle and in the absolute rejection of the conventional regiments of supernumeraries who people the court of Denmark on stage.

But perhaps the boldest experiments with decor have been on the Soviet stage. Already in 1901, Lensky, the famous Russian producer, wrote: 'The painted scene is not to be regarded as a thing apart but as standing in relation to the piece for which it was painted . . . Painting in the theatre is merely part of a complicated organism creating the unity of the production.'

Thus we see the irrelevance of the proscenium arch. And pre-fabricated housing plans on stage had been realized and condemned before the Soviet revolutionaries stormed the theatre. But the Lenskian constructivists advocated the simplification of decor within very narrow limits and that too, only for preserving the supremacy of literature over scenic design. With the Soviet era began a struggle for popular art, and a long process of growth culminated in the modern highly complicated science of a people's theatre.

Among the most outstanding Shakespeare presentations by Russia is the Moscow Art Theatre production of *Twelfth Night*. Vladimir Favorsky, who did the decor, designed the city of Illyria on a toy-scale, squeezed into the periphery of a small stage, and the actors towered over spires and towers and rooftops like giants. At every step Favorsky consciously and deliberately refused to give any impression; across the black cloth, painted into a sky over the toy-world, ran a stream with the word 'Illyria' scrawled across it. The actors therefore moved about in surroundings produced by the poetic imagination, making it clear to the audience that the toy-world was only an excuse for the impossible world of Shakespeare's intellect.

Nisson Shifrin struck home in *The Taming of the Shrew* by making Petruchio and Katherina go round and round on merry-go-round horses, making us delightfully aware of the childishness in men and women. (The British production, with modern costumes for Petruchio and Katherina, was an effort on similar lines.) Shifrin was also responsible for turning the wood in *A Midsummer Night's Dream*—all the trees and logs and bushes—into many fairies at the end of the play.

The principle of identifying the stage property with the actor is brought out very consistently in Alexander Tyshler's decor of *Richard III*—the padded walls of the castle are reflected exactly in the padded armour of Richmond's men who storm it. Thus Favorsky and Tyshler have given to the world two different methods of relating the actor to the set. Favorsky juxtaposes two contrasts: the living form of the actor and the unreal image of Illyria. Tyshler identifies two similars: the padded warrior and the padded castle. Both, however, occuring at the transition period of the Soviet stage, agreed in the outright rejection of illusionistic realism.

We come now to direction. Obviously, directors must always look at each medium at their disposal for production as a whole. It is alleged by the director that Shakespeare is very often box-office poison, unless backed by triumphant spectacles and tableaux. *Henry V* was on the verge of being banned in USA, just as the British experts condemned Soviet pictures. But once the monstrous expenditure on gigantic stage productions is drastically cut down, the director will find he has saved enough money to put across two more Shakespeare plays. Thus, he will be able to produce three instead of one.

The risk of pecuniary flop gone, the director will be able to approach his tasks more in the spirit of art. He will then feel the need to *interpret* Shakespeare, not merely give a running commentary on a medieval theme. But he must see to it that his work does not become an aimless, and, above all, useless adventure. Like his fellow artistes, the writer, the poet or the musician, the director too has a social responsibility to fulfil—to entertain and to educate.

What is there to educate in Shakespeare? In the Elizabethan Age, the passage of time was sluggish pace; up to the 1890s, time carried on at an unostentatious pace. But in this century time is advancing at cosmic speed. Events splash across the world's newspapers. Many find reason to believe in a worldwide transition towards a better society. At this juncture, men and women, fatigued with struggle, hunger to be reassured of the values we have spoken about. These values have to be presented to them again, so that they may resolve the conflict and engage in struggle again.

Shakespeare, therefore, wrote his plays at a time when the pace of life was slower, hence his own mode of presentation. And we, of this faster age, must have ours. So the director must remember two points with regard to the spectator he is educating: first, the average citizen is already embittered with struggle and expects to see a simplified world on the stage. He wants to see all his feelings reflected in the play and he wants to be given a solution, but not on the complicated and painful plane of his day-to-day life. He must also feel somehow heightened through his appreciation of the play's peculiar realism. So all art must be elevating. Secondly, in order to drive home the contents of the play, the director must disarm the prejudices of a modern crowd.

The first can be achieved by an austere simplicity of presentation —completely doing away with supernumeraries and gorgeous scenery. In the last century, perhaps, it was possible to devote time to flounder endlessly in needless masquerades and highly technical fencing bouts. Now, when poetry itself, under the impact of speed, has acquired a journalistic attitude, drama, which is nothing but a chapter of life analysed within limits, has barely the scope to state the essentials. This brings us to the second point: to drive the content home, the director is not obliged to stop at anything, be it a film-projector, a mike or an unconventional stage-composition.

Conservatives, who are unscrupulous enough to reduce drama by means of scenic realism to the level of the cinematograph, oppose the use of such new machinery on the basis of the sanctity of the stage and its appliances. True, the film projector and the mike have not yet become conventional stage appliances but, only the other day, the curtain was not a proper device and the box stage was a sacrilege. These have now been accepted because they facilitated an understanding of the thematic power in plays. Similarly Othello's emotions, the triangle between his wife, Iago and Cassio which he conjures up, can be much more convincingly portrayed with a film projection of three heads revolving round and round, with Othello's troubled voice heard over the microphone.

We come now to the actor. When he takes his place on the stage, he is an unexploited concept of life. He has within him the power of exploiting himself, provided his own interpretation, his own ideas of acting, scenic design and interpretation are not repressed by the dictatorship of an autocratic director. In collective direction, he will have his say regarding the production as a whole and will not fail to make for himself, in an accommodating way, those provisions which are essential for the revelation of his mental working. Of course, it must be repeated that such a departure from the conventional mode of directorial monarchy will depend entirely on the ability and willingness of the actors to cooperate as artistes in human history in a spirit of sacrifice to the other media of the theatre and for his fellow actor.

The decline of interest in Shakespeare in our times has been brought about by the attempt to restrict him to the confines of the leisured class. This is to be combated by re-establishing the link between Shakespeare and life, not Elizabethan life, but ours—the life which alone, therefore, can breathe health and future into the art of Shakespeare which is dying in the hands of a few.

(*The Sunday Statesman*, 24 July 1949.
Reproduced in *Epic Theatre*, March 1998.)

Oedipus Wrecked

There can be only three ways of approaching the classics in modern theatre: firstly, by presenting them purely from a dramatic standpoint, in which case a detailed representation of ancient Greek customs, rituals and conventions, as well as accurate costuming and decor are called for; secondly, by adopting a historical attitude and trying to recapture the conventions of Dionysian theatre; thirdly, a poetic approach, which can discard most trappings and focus on presenting the power of early drama through verse and symbols.

In the production of *Oedipus Rex* by Bohurupee, the third approach—the poetic—has obviously been deliberately jettisoned. Because, in spite of a great deal of energetic articulation, the translation is utterly flat and prosaic. One can only conclude that it is deliberate, for nothing else can explain the nonchalance towards the poetry of Sophocles. In the long reported-speech (*oratio oblique*) narratives, Greek excels all other languages except perhaps Sanskrit. This is because any Greek grammar, however elementary, will teach the aorist participle which, in Greek, conveys aspect and not the rigid pastness that the English participle indicates. This is a form close to Bengali and makes Sophocles easier to adapt from the original. The middle voice, so rare in English, is another prop of the indirect-speech narrative in Greek drama which Bengali can adopt without distortion. But obviously an English translation has intervened here, and Sombhu Mitra, translator, has had to drop poetry and approach each speech purely from the viewpoint of theatrical effectiveness.

The second approach—recapturing the theatre of Sophocles's time—is evidently beyond the capacity of Bohurupee, or any other group in the country. What with masks and *cothurni*, *skemata* and *skene*, the strict adherence to the rules of the Chorus, which must sing and dance, such a project becomes Greek to those who will play and those who will watch. Further, research will have to be made into *melapoeia*, that strange ancient science of music, with its acutes, graves and circumflexes.

The only approach left—that of presenting Sophocles in his real historical setting—cannot be so simple either, because it involves a fantastic amount of research. And one is not sure whether filling the Sophoclean world with supernumeraries and brass pots and tumble-down loggias on a Theban street will not destroy Sophocles himself. This approach further involves a kind of acting that is surcharged with emotion and one wonders whether that too will not come into conflict with the poise and composure of a Greek classic.

Modern research has placed Sophocles, Aeschylus and Euripides in close proximity with the rituals of Eleusian belief and the Pythagorean fraternity. The festival dramatists, when they talked of Zeus and the Olympians, did not mean the happy-go-lucky drunken human gods whom it was possible to love and hate but referred obliquely to the death rituals whence Dionysus had sprung. It was not a bacchanalia but an appeal to mysterious subconscious feelings associated with the worship of the dead. The top of Dionysus's temple rising over the Athenian theatre further underlined the ritual nature of these plays; it was a dramatic celebration of a communal ecstasy based on fear.

Hence, inexonerably, Greek drama and its theatre become grave, solemn, like the marble whereof they carve the image of Dionysus. The Chorus and its leader, the *koripheos*, shatter the action whenever it tends to grow out of ritual and threatens to become real. Their *parodos*, *strophes* and *antistrophes* serve more than a moral purpose, and their ritual function is equally important. The gestures and movements of the actors and the Chorus are broad, vast, slow, because, as Raymond Williams points out, 'the purpose of any movement (in the Greek theatre) is mimetic—that is to say, the physical realization of what is being verbally expressed'. Nothing else can explain the convention of the *skemata*, of the slow rhythmic dance of the 15 choristers to accompany the *stasimon*, of the participation of the Chorus in the action itself with momentous gestures in the *orkesis*.

Bohurupee, baffled by the conflict between convention and what they consider dramatic, decided to infuse everything and everybody with nervous excitement and emotion. Not even the Chorus, in their pronouncements on the power of destiny, were spared this hysteria. The result was consistently peevish, often ludicrous. The king and the queen, in the throes of doubt, behaved normally—as normally as schoolchildren in love.

Sophocles's text was supposed to inspire the actor to a kind of religious discipline, where the folds of the cloak and the height of the actor on his wooden shoes, helped by an immovable mask, would make of him a statue. But then the audience will not know the difference, because the ring, the sound quality of Sophocles's text, has been carefully suppressed in this version. Otherwise the conflict between its 'choral' quality (for want of a better word) and the peevish acting would have hit the audience as strongly as if a twist had been danced to Beethoven's Ninth. This is the little dishonesty of the production—it is not a historical attitude we see here, nor a respect for Sophocles's poetry, nor even a make-shift arrangement to replace Sophocles to our time. Bohurupee has taken from Sophocles whatever lay within its reach—everything else could go to blazes. The company has attempted to 'stylize' a bit by flinging its arms about. Hence, everyone on the stage, except Mitra, looks demented, and the lean arms shoot about as if to drive away the flies. It has tried to 'stylize' the set too: a couple of offensive red pillars with a crude symbol of Phoebus on the arch that reeks of the symbolism of *Raktakarabi* and merely convinces us that a bare stage would be a lot better.

We put this proposition squarely to Bohurupee: if you want a 'stylized' production which will avoid the problems of our time, create your own plays. But, for heaven's sake, if you try Sophocles, be honest with him. A lot more responsibility devolves on a group when it tries a Greek play, because, apart from the core of universal truth, all the other aspects have lost their validity for a modern audience. To explain them away by pretending that they are merely the emotive outpourings of tortured souls is to be dishonest to dramatist and audience alike.

It would be interesting to know why *Oedipus* was selected, jumping over time and ignoring the thousands of years in between, why Moliére, Shakespeare or Goethe were not considered worthy of attention if foreign classics were to be adapted at all. We remember the Bengali pun with which Mr Mitra used to equate Bengali productions of foreign classics with 'monkeying'. It is good to see he has changed his views. But, then, why *Oedipus*? Because, said the advertisement once, 'it is a play of darkness'. Naturally, Aristophanes would be too close to social criticism, as would Shakespeare, Molière, Goethe and other rabble-rousers. But *Oedipus* itself, in spite of its insistence on 'darkness' and 'the burden of the past' on the human soul, remind us sternly and repeatedly of the welfare of the commonwealth. After all, the Greek audiences loved their commonwealth and their religion with a passion that modern 'honest' *régisseur*s could do well to well learn from.

In spite of all this, one may declare, without hesitation or reserve, that Sombhu Mitra is the greatest actor of the present Indian theatre. There is no one within miles of this man in speech or economy of gesture. He is the only one in the cast who achieved the impossible: he almost convinced me that Sophocles really wrote a bit of intense drama about an ancient Hamlet. But the others dutifully scuttled Mitra's scheme. Jocasta was an insult to the audience's sensitivity. It is time we realized that different characters have different attitudes, and all need not be played like a tipsy Harlem accoster. Tiresias mistook Sophocles for D. L. Roy, and the old men, for no fault of theirs but by the absurdity of making the Chorus real men of flesh and blood, were ridiculous. Creon spoke well and moved badly. Two better performances came at the end—Laius's former slave and the Second Messenger. Tapas Sen's brilliant lighting tries to retrieve a lost position by an ominous darkening when the Fates are mentioned.

Just a word on the pronunciation of nominatives, of which Bohurupee takes commendable care. 'Oidipous' in Greek is not pronounced as if the first syllable becomes a dipthong ('way'), a fault almost the whole cast keeps making. The *omicron* and the *iota* must be kept separate. The second syllable, '*pous*', is not to be widened to rhyme with 'louse' but the *omicron* and *upsilon* must be pronounced together, with an accented lengthening of the vowel. If, further, such care is bestowed on the name of the protagonist, why should

Corinthos be spared? And the *theta* of Thebai? And why should 'Teire-sias' be rendered thus, with a German dipthong in the first syllable?

(Written under the pseudonym Iago in
Now, 30 October 1964.)

The Calcutta Stage

The importance of professional theatre in Calcutta can only be assessed if one remembers that the five of them [theatre-houses] together play to about 70,000 people every month. At the end of a year, the figure becomes fantastic. This is a region where the great IPTA made no headway at all. The first break occurred only five years ago; otherwise, the tycoons have been left free to peddle the worst brands of superstition. The luxurious Star Theatre specializes in the woman question and its findings insult every liberty that our women have attained so far. Its stories usually revolve around the devoted wife, whose husband drinks, beats her and runs off with another woman. But the wife's devotion is proof against all trials and she usually dies in the last scene, with her hand on the prodigal husband's feet. The mythical Code Bill is made mincemeat of.

Biswaroopa, that other citadel of monetary approach to theatre, has just finished a thousand-night run of *Setu* (Bridge, 1959)—an incredible rigmarole about a woman who finds her stomach growing larger and larger, and cannot decide whether it is a child or a tumour. She occasionally, without apparent reason, tries to kill herself under a train, so that Tapas Sen may work wonders with his lights. The woman was played hysterically, intolerably, unpardonably by Tripti Mitra. Biswaroopa's present venture *Lagna* (The Auspicious Moment) defies description. Its infantile set is being advertised as 'theatrescope'—whatever that may mean—and is an amateurish imitation of what has been tried and rejected by theatres 20 years ago. That does not prevent the management from peddling its wares as 'invented' (English never being the strong point of our theatre tycoons) by one Rashbehari Sarker.

Rangmahal hit the headlines when the actors went on a stay-in strike to prevent the owners from turning it into a cinema hall. The settlement enabled the actors to take over the theatre, but under an unfair agreement. However, their struggle continues to keep the theatre running and, even at their worst, they are far above the meanness of the other commercial productions. Their current play is an adaptation of Oscar Wilde.

Mukta Angan, built manually by members of Shouvanik with the object of producing plays in the tradition of the new theatre movement, seems to have passed into the hands of philistines who are currently butchering Shakespeare. Their production of *Othello* in Bengali is to be seen to be believed.

Minerva, run by the Little Theatre Group, still tries to bring the toiling masses onto the stage by telling their stories and making them the heroes of their plays. But, of course, a violent press campaign against them has become a permanent feature. Hooligans raided the theatre during the playing of *Angar* and stopped it. The theatre was raided again during the communal riots in January for the crime of rescuing Muslim victims of mob violence. The Theatre Centre was burnt down recently by an accidental fire.

But the real theatre in Calcutta, since the IPTA splintered into several inspired groups, is the non-commercial theatre. What has overtaken them today that they cannot even remember for whom they are supposed to play? That they have forgetten that a people's theatre not only stars the people but is meant for the people?

There is a spate of foreign plays on our stage at the moment. The selection is random. A group has currently made a success of Pirandello's *Six Characters*, though the play may not be suitable for a people's theatre movement. Another group, a very capable one, has selected *Waiting for Godot* and announces boldly that the play deals with the collapse of bourgeois morals after the war. Beckett himself would sue the producers for libel if he came to know of it. To Beckett, man is a moron, and life is a glimmer of light enclosed by darkness. To foist a fictitious reading on him and to try to make him a revolutionary is an infantile attempt to deceive the audience. But the audience is not deceived. The whole play—every line, every situation, every confrontation—belies the 'Marxist' protagonists of this otherwise powerful group. It is significant that Brecht, Whiting Wester, Hochhuth, even Dürrenmatt, remain untouched.

Rupakar has buried itself in *Byapika Viday* (Farewell to the Brazen Hussy), a pointless farce by Amritalal. This group relies on a brilliant singer who also directs; therefore, he cannot select or make good a play that has not a male singing part in it. But the question is: though we must respect the classics, why should we pick on the most reactionary examples of our old theatre? The same goes for Chaturanga's *Baboo* by Amritalal. It is time Amritalal was given a decent burial, along with his violent prejudices of class, caste and religion. Thrillers are in vogue too; a group's plagiarized version of the American trash *Chase a Crooked Shadow* has made quite a hit.

Coming to Bohurupee, one enters a higher plane. There is nothing slipshod here, neither in production nor in selection of plays. We have seen them do Sophocles, Tagore and Ibsen with a fluency that any group in the world might envy. But a lot of whimwham is being raised by this group about 'honest' plays and 'dishonest' ones. To whom, according to them, must the theatre movement be honest? The answer was given a long time ago by the parent body from which Bohurupee sprang: honest to the people. But by their exclusive audience (due to the location of their theatre) and their fanatical insistence on the classics, the group has already retreated from the people and increasingly grows anaemic and haughty. They are trying to be honest merely to themselves, and will inevitably retire into experiment for experiment's sake. That they are not always honest to the theatre movement is obvious because it is this group that agitates for an end to the expression 'the new theatre movement'. Naturally, having discarded genuine people from their audience, having discarded plays on contemporary themes, they cannot do otherwise.

There is a minor group, the Theatre Unit, whose director showed exceptional clarity of vision as regards the aims and objects of the theatre movement. But today there is a shocking discrepancy in the group's words and deeds. In a recent article, the director summarized his views on the current theatre movement and it is amazing how his group's activities contradict every sentence. He heaps abuse on producing Amritalal; his group plays Amritalal's *Kripaner Dhan* (The Miser's Fortune). He rails against producing Shakespeare, irrespective of whether it is his centenary year or the fact that he is more modern than many modern playwrights or that his group joined the official celebration of the Shakespeare quarter-centenary with a shoddy production of *Julius Caesar*. He demands that only the most militant plays be produced for genuine audiences; his group's repertoire rests on Maugham's mystic *Sheppey* and that most decadent of all farces, *Charley's Aunt*. He rails against Shakespeare and Sophocles because they are old and cannot meet the militant demands of the people; his group regularly plays *Mrichhakatika*.

What should be the theatre movement's attitude to the classics? Firstly, the classics cannot replace plays on current problems. If a group were to restrict itself to the classics and exclude modern drama, it cannot claim that it has advanced the cause of the theatre. Secondly, all classics cannot be produced on the contemporary stage; one must select vigilantly. Thirdly, today only the theatre movement can rescue the classics from oblivion and it is its sacred duty to do so, instead of leaving them to commercial manipulators who distort and castrate them. Dash Rupak Group has managed to do just that in its attempt to revive *Raja Ravana*—it is an insult to intelligence.

What are the three fundamental principles of the People's Theatre movement? Let us repeat them because so many seem to forget them: first, the toiling people must be the heroes of drama; second, the toiling people must be the audience of drama; third, experiment in form must be at the level of the audience, i.e. the toilers. One group alone, the Rupantari, appears to adhere firmly to these principles. Their brilliant production of *Karnik*—the story of masons—as well as their prompt play against communal terror in January confirms our faith in them.

An interesting development of the theatre movement is the living newspaper—squads of actors playing in street corners, *bastis* and villages, on day-to-day issues that affect the life of the people. At such performances, the actor stands in the middle of his audience, undisturbed by prosceniums and lights, and a communion is forged which strengthens the theatre movement. Out of such enterprises are shaped the sinews of a democratic culture in the heart of the audience.

(Written under the pseudonym Iago in *Now*, 6 November 1964.)

Sartre's Choice

To the independent-minded, the Nobel Prize has always appeared to be somewhat of a contradiction. It violates the militant freedom that writers in the Western world profess with such enthusiasm. It appears to measure their achievements in terms of cash and undermines their talk of 'not by bread alone'. It appears to provide them with nothing but bread. And consider the prizes for literature—and the ignominy of Lagerkirst being bracketed with Churchill. The Peace Prize has, of course, always been the laughing stock of the world, because the Norwegian Sorting Committee which recommends it considers Schweitzer and Cordell Hull to be on the same level. Jean-Paul Sartre has administered a shock therapy that is not likely to affect the Stockholm Academy.

However, Sartre has done his duty. Ever since he broke decisively with his own *L'Etre et le Néant* (*Being and Nothingness*, 1943), and began to advocate works that present questions in 'the most radical and intransigent manner', he has been subjected to humiliating abuse by Claude Simon and Yves Berger & Co. But his advance from *Crime Passionnel* (1948)—a vitriolic, anti-Soviet tirade—to Nekrassov is the measure of his abandonment of Husserl, and of his political commitment. Simon cannot stand Sartre's call to writers to side tendentiously, radically and militantly, with the two million starving. Nor can he reconcile himself to Sartre's latest attempts to study dialectics and his choice of Marx over Heidegger. For this man is responsible for the phrase 'hell is other people'.

It is Sartre who once considered life to be an 'ineffective passion'. It is he who condemned his Orestes to an inevitable visitation of the flies. His Garcin was trying—in vain—to make an effective exit from a life lived in cowardice. His Mathieu never found the answer to a single question, and therefore lived for himself. Mathieu became free merely because he no longer lived *in* himself.

An omnipotent presence of death has always dominated the older Sartre, a narrow life within which to make a choice and achieve a purpose—both to be destroyed by death. Kierkegaard and Heidegger had found an atheist messiah. For this other Sartre, one could have admiration because he confirmed that revolution is a waste of time, that the Marxist ideal of controlling nature and society is unrealistic. He robbed man of his confidence and comfort—that was a great comfort. But now this playboy of anti-Soviet hysteria has become a Frankenstein. He condemns French terror in Algeria and Vietnam, but coolly defends Soviet action in Hungary and the Chinese takeover of Tibet. This man is no longer non-aligned. When he portrayed Communists as professional thugs and the Soviet Union as an imperialist power—that was true freedom of the writer. Now Oliver has turned vicious. Naturally Simon must say, 'This man has now turned rich from the sale of his books and can afford to turn politician.' M. Simon cannot see beyond his pocket because M. Simon is free and non-aligned. Boris Pasternak—it is now an axiom—refused the prize because the OGPU (Ob'edinennoe Gosudarstvennoe Politicheskoe Upravlenie/The State Directorate)—or its Khruschevite parallel—held a Mauser to his head.

Shaw declined because he was a maniacal egotist—an image built up for us through years of persistent propaganda. But now Sartre. It is difficult to conceive of any cloak-and-dagger goings-on which could force him to it in broad daylight in Paris. On the other hand, not being an existentialist any more, he could not have gone eccentric. The only conclusion—that he exercised free choice—is rather frightening for free artistes.

Mathieu has made his choice. Probably unknown to himself, Sartre too made it a long time ago, in the heyday of his isolationist philosophy, because Garcin suddenly says, in contradiction to his entire attitude, 'Each man has an aim in life, a leading motive: that's so, isn't it? Well, I didn't give a damn for wealth, or for love. I aimed at being a real man. A tough, as they say' (*No Exit*, 1944).

(Written under the pseudonym Iago in
Now, 6 November 1964.)

Little Theatricals

The year 1964 has been an extremely busy one for the Little Theatre Group of Calcutta. In this year, they have played their two old hits *Angar* (Coal, 1959) and *Titash Ekti Nadir Naam* (A River Called Titash, 1963) countless times and presented Shakespeare's *Othello*, *Julius Caesar*, *Romeo and Juliet* and *A Midsummer Night's Dream*, as well as, very recently, Friedrich Wolf's *Professor Mamlock* (1933). Of all these new plays, only *Othello* was in English; the rest were in Bengali. It is time someone reviewed their work critically and roused in their director, Mr Utpal Dutt, a balance and humility that he seems to lack of late.

Of *Angar*: pages have been written in many journals all over India, many of them condemnatory on flimsy political grounds. Some have attacked the production on the plea that undue importance has been attached to lighting and decor. I do not agree with this criticism, because subterranean galleries in a coalmine require a tremendous amount of atmosphere, and a modern *régisseur* will naturally take recourse to mechanical devices. I challenge the play itself. Author Utpal Dutt has conceived a lower-middle-class world, with its cheap sentimentality and romanticism, and passed it off as a document of proletarian life. To crown it all, the play develops into the moribund formula of the mother–son relationship and stumbles into the same morass of East-Lynnism which has plagued our theatre for a hundred years now.

Mr Utpal Dutt's adaptation of *Titash Ekti Nadir Naam*, one of the outstanding novels of the century, is an example of superficial theatricality intruding on and destroying literature. It is strange that the critics in the city have been so dazzled by the flamboyant production of the play that they have failed to notice the mess that has been made of the original. The novel is elemental in passionate power, and the madness, murder and fights are spread over an enormous space. Cramped into a three-hour play, we are treated to an unending series of violence and are reminded of Micky Spillane. The gangway in the auditorium is defiantly experimental and is pulled off mainly by the group's sound teamwork. But can that blind us to the absurdity of the fair scene where strange characters invade the stage and fantastic events take place, quite unknown to the original? As for the river scene: both Mr Dutt and Mr Tapas Sen stand indicted on a charge of slighting the audience's intelligence.

Coming to Shakespeare: let us begin by congratulating the group on important pioneering work. But, of course, the token performance of *Othello* in English—repeated several times to packed houses—was a sorry affair. The text was mangled so unscrupulously that the great second scene was out and 'improvements' were made on Shakespeare's arrangement of events in Act III. Mr Dutt as Othello was rather a pitiable sight, with his voice gone, his breathing laboured and his bulk enormous; who can pardon his puffing and blowing in the 'Pontic sea' and 'Farewell the tranquil mind' speeches? Desdemona, looking very pretty, stumbled all over the stage as well as her lines, and made it quite obvious that her ability was no match for her enthusiasm. Iago looked like a character out of *Tom Brown's Schooldays*, bullying little fags at the top of his voice and headed inexorably for the headmaster's strap on his backside. Cassio looked like his favourite fag, and Bianca spoke a language quite impossible to understand as English.

Presenting Shakespeare in Bengali has always been Mr Dutt's forte and his version of *Caesar* in fascist uniform—a very old fashion, for the information of those who hailed it as an innovation—was quite enough to raise a miniature cyclone in our complacent world. Everyone began to chime with an opinion or two on this 'pseudo-Marxist' outrage; most of these critics never even saw the production and some have never heard of modern-dress productions of Shakespeare. I consider this slick brown-shirted *Caesar* to be the Little Theatre Group's best production to date, in spite of the fact that we could not hear a word that Brutus said.

But the appalling *Romeo and Juliet*! Will Mr Dutt pause long enough to admit that it is idiotic to cut the play almost down to half? That, once the play-fever is upon him, he assumes the form of a demon who has scant respect for any playwright, even Shakespeare? We saw some well-executed fencing, some well-dressed men and women, a competent Romeo and a sinister tomb-scene decor. For the rest, Mr Dutt's blind gallop ended in Gilpinesque retribution. We even saw actors forget to bring props on and knock their hats off amidst their violent gestures. Mr Dutt's own Mercutio, he will agree, is best forgotten, and both Juliet and Tybolt had better go back to intensive training.

The *Dream* was infinitely superior, especially in terms of acting, with Oberon, Titania, Puck, the lovers and the rude mechanicals all doing robust work. But once more we are forced to harp on the text and demand of Mr Dutt whether he has been accurate and faithful to the original right through. For example, does he feel that he has correctly rendered Titania's speech, 'His mother was a votress of my order'? Or does his knowledge of English not permit anything better? The play within the play was so overlaid with slapstick that one began to doubt whether these were Shakespeare's fools, or escaped tricksters from a music hall.

The latest production—Wolf's *Professor Mamlock*, translated, once more by Mr Dutt, into Bengali—scores through a startling topicality that hits the audience in the face; with very minor changes, the play could have been a record of recent events and trends in this country. But Mr Dutt's insistence on keeping the locale German and the period early thirties I find entirely unconvincing. I cannot accept the whitened face of Mr Dutt as that of a Jewish doctor in terror of fascism. For similar reasons, I cannot swallow Rolf, Inge, Hirsh and Karlsen. The two glorious exceptions were the terror-stricken Ruth Mamlock and Werner Seidel with his Trotskyish beard.

However, *Mamlock* is a production that pulls no punches and speaks frankly on vital subjects. Once upon a time we were used to this kind of aggressive work by the Little Theatre Group and I, for one, rejoiced in their courage of conviction. Currently, loaded with a home of its own, the group has probably to be careful, and the general offensive it faced did it no good either. But it is heartening to see it has not gone under. *Mamlock* retrieves the position it had lost with the demoralizing last scene of *Titash*. In order to advance further, the director will have to shed a lot of his browbeating arrogance and recognize the need for humility. Amen.

(Written under the pseudonym Iago in *Now*, 27 November 1964.)

Death of a Salesman

It was fun watching Calcutta's leading daily make quixotic comments on the Dramatic Club's [of Calcutta; DCC] latest production *The Death of a Salesman*, trying to prove that Arthur Miller was a 'non-writer'. If the critic is certain that Miller's only preoccupation was to get married to Marilyn, he might at least have had the decency to be quiet and concentrate on *Dear Charles* and other nonsense that the DCC has for long inflicted upon us and which are definitely more suited to his intelligence.

For perhaps the first time—barring a couple of attempts at Shakespeare and Shaw—the DCC has thrilled the audience with serious drama, seriously produced and acted. For the first time, the DCC has jettisoned its usual fare of drawing-room imbecility, and the result no doubt went over the head of the daily's esteemed critic. He probably discovered in the play secret attempts to place a time-bomb directly under the rotunda of the Writers' Building. It might satisfy his conscience to know that this play, hailed by Franco's Spain, was for long under a virtual ban in the USSR. It might further inspire him in the right direction to learn—if he thinks Albee is a 'writer' and is advancing the American theatre—that some have even thought the pen stolen by Biff an eloquent phallic symbol.

This fury, albeit uninformed, is understandable. The play generates vague uncomfortable feelings in the same way as does *Hamlet*, which operates simultaneously at two levels—there is a rotten Denmark and there is a complex mind on the borderline of madness. There is a stark social world full of greed and the struggle for existence, where to be old is to be destroyed. This becomes evident while Howard listens to his daughter's whistling and Bernard packs his tennis racquet for a trip to Washington. There is the other world of Willy's mind. The play was originally called *The Inside of His Head*, implying a mind already in the twilight of consciousness where reality ceases to exist and eerie shadows walk in frightening succession. Willy Loman is driven to his madness; it does not just nip in on a social visit. He was riding on a smile and a shoeshine, but society does not play him fair. Ben sums up the philosophy of the asphalt jungle—'Never fight fair with a stranger, boy. You'll never get out of the jungle that way.' And Xerxes Mehta's interpretation of the name Loman points to the universality of the character from the Kleine Man in Brecht's *Schweyk* to Chaplin's little tramp, and, cutting across continents, disturbs the tea-room quietude of Calcutta's cultured aristocracy.

The principal production hurdle in *Salesman* is to distinguish, without making it obvious or naive, between reality and the shadows of the past. It would be the easiest gimmick in the world for any stage manager to transfer the illusion sequences to an inner stage behind a net, and present Ben and the fragments of the past in a haze of cloudy shapes. And in that we would inevitably have watched the destruction of Miller's intentions, for he has presented the experiences of a salesman, his past and his present, his mind and his daily life, not separately, not even in parallel lines, but in a parcel, in a block, in portmanteau. They are as inextricably woven together as Hamlet's feigned madness and real melancholy.

Miller, criticizing the film adaptation of this play, blamed its failure (it wasn't such a failure, was it?) on the fact that the so-called flashbacks were presented full-scale, with Loman being physically transported to those surroundings. Thus, thinks Miller, present horrors were drained from his family life and the play was torn to bits. It is difficult to please a playwright with a film version of his own work. But it is true that, in the film, in the shadowy world of Loman's imagination, he seemed to exist alone. Neither Linda, nor Biff nor Happy could take part in it because the actuality of the flashback, the fading-out of the house and the slow fade-in of other sets, forbade their meddling and ignored their feelings. The flashbacks seemed mere episodes from the past that any normal man may remember at moments of stress. The terrifying abnormality of Willy Loman, surrounded by real, anxious and dear people and yet living a life where they cannot help, is lost in the film. The horror of a man disintegrating before your eyes is the real power of this play. And you are uncomfortably reminded of the many battered individuals you meet on the road who talk to themselves.

Mr Xerxes Mehta made the action glide so smoothly from reality to illusion and back again that there was no artificial separation. He did it principally by the simple but stirring trick of making the actors walk through the imaginary front wall of the house and emerge into what is supposed to be the garden. But when real, they would walk round to the front door. Coupled with it was Mr Tapas Sen's lighting which changed just perceptibly to suggest the move to another plane. His lighting of Willy in his shirt-sleeves looking up in awe at Ben's imperious umbrella was a masterpiece in dramatic lighting. So was the golden light that suddenly lit up the murky world as Willy and his sons shouted the triumph of Loman's enterprise.

Mr Mehta's set closely followed that of the original American production. It was the wisest thing to do for want of a revolving stage. I, for one, have always imagined the rooms spread out along the circumference of a stage and the motion of the stage picking up speed as we near the end, adding another dimension to the play. It would visually represent a whirling world of diseased fantasy and the speed of a world going about its business, with Willy Loman in the centre of it all. In short, for both the principal aspects of the play, a turn-table would lend itself to the most creative use. This play, more than any other, requires a moving set.

However, Mr Xerxes Mehta, with Mr Christopher Richardson and Mr Tapas Sen, was able to create an atmosphere of overcrowding, poverty and insecurity in the tiered set, and he made his cast play with all their muscles taut with nervous excitement. Whenever Biff met Willy, it was jungle war—no give and no take, no quarter asked. It was the replica of the world where the weaker has to go under. Underlying the social symbolism is the fact that both Willy and Biff are neurotic, psychological victims of social insecurity. Therefore, when they fight, they fight like mad men, and there is no Osric to cry 'nothing either way', because they are incensed and will not be parted.

Terrence Rochford as Willy Loman was an amazing study in all these subtle shades of *dementia praecox*, and yet he gave every move, every business and every word such control and dignity that Loman becomes not pitiable (who would pity this man?), but towering, huge.

You want to respect him. You want him to die at the end so that he can escape the ignominy of being a burden to his people. You understand him, though Linda does not. Mainly through Rochford's complex, powerful study of Loman, Mr Mehta arrives at Miller's intention to write a high tragedy about the common man. One does not have to be a prince, says Miller, to be a tragic hero, and the fall of the hero need not be measured on the social scale. But how easy it is to make of the butler a clown! How easily Pinter's lower middle class becomes ridiculous! Even the university professor in Edward Albee's *Who's Afraid of Virginia Woolf* looks a pleasant lunatic, barely worthy of notice. To create a tragic hero from the masses of workmen and salesmen requires a John Steinbeck or an Arthur Miller. Terence Rochford, an amateur who can teach many Indian professionals a trick or two, raises Loman to this tragic dignity.

He is brilliantly supported by Sheila Ma_____, especially when she tries to sing him to sleep, when she talks of the length of pipe in the cellar, when she telephones Biff thinking it is Willy who has put it away and when she finally turns on her sons and defends Willy. Biff, ably played by Derek Roberts, need not have planted his feet so wide apart every time he is aggressive, which is naturally very frequent. This bit of awkwardness and his uniformly high-pitched voice interfered with our understanding of Biff's psychology. Too much externalizing reduces depth, and we come away with the impression that Biff is not so much plagued by the troubles of the brain nor rooted sorrow in his memory, as by a naturally aggressive and maniacal character. However, when he weeps on his brother's shoulder, he superbly compensates. Peter Lancaster's happy Happy was most enjoyable; but, of course, Basil Gill's Ben and Nick Northover's Howard grab all the kudos for minor parts, the other minors looking like inarticulate shadows beside them. I feel Ben should not be dressed like a prospector, but a millionaire with diamond rings and a cigar. It is not his adventures that haunt Willy but the fact that he was a success, that he made it and that he got rich.

In the general warfare between Biff and Willy—uniformly violent and brilliantly directed—there was just one significant line thrown away that should not have been. We could hardly hear Biff's 'Since when did you get so clean?' in the turmoil. I believe Mr Mehta should have given it pauses before and after and let it fall with crippling violence on Willy (who explodes only because he realizes its gruesome truth). He should have stuck it in our memory. It is the only line that gives us a hint as to why Willy and Biff fight like animals. We would have remembered it in the terrible hotel scene in Boston and been chilled by the memory.

These are, however, minor points. Xerxes Mehta and his cast have taken me by storm. They have turned the tide that was threatening to drown the DCC into a cesspool of decadence and rot. The flowers that Linda places outside the curtain-line, over the imaginary grave of her husband, hold for us a very special significance. They are Ophelia's rosemary for remembrance. (If only Tapas Sen had kept his spot on them until after Curtain.) We shall remember. And we shall hope for new productions—not of little lambs eating ivy, but of time being out of joint and defiance of augury.

(Written under the pseudonym Iago.
Now, 4 December 1964.)

MYTHMAKERS

It was difficult conducting Candide through the History Congress, because he has the irritating attitude of letting his lower jaw droop and batting his eyelids in furious imitation of a naval signal-light. Stranger still, the single wisp of hair on his head nods in agreement. He seems perpetually astonished, even at the fact that he is alive.

A speaker had just made the stirring remark, 'India has always taught the world the ideal of peace and friendship.' At this, Candide halted and began his facial acrobatics. 'That's odd,' he said, 'that's really odd, you know.'

'And why?' said I. 'Let's push along, Candide, there are other committees in session. Nice ones.'

'No, but this—' said he, not moving an inch, ' "India has always taught the world . . ." What world? When did she teach? How old is she?'

Damned if I know, I vaguely recalled some energetic quarrel between the Thingummies and the So-and-So's about whether the Vedas were written in BC 3000 or 200. As if it makes a difference.

'No doubt she is very old,' said Candide. 'Those Egyptologists and Sinologists—crass ignorant lot, you know. India must be older than the world, because she taught it.'

This was highbrow stuff. So I shot at him what I was fairly sure of: 'You've heard of Angkor Them?'

'Yes, no doubt I have.'

'QED India taught 'em. Taught 'em good and proper!'

For a whole minute Candide pondered over this. 'You've heard no doubt,' he finally said, 'of Gandhara art?'

Had I? May as well fight on. 'Of course. Who hasn't?'

'That's Greek, you know', he said.

'QED Greece taught India. How simple history sounds when you come to this country.' He was genuinely delighted.

But the speaker in the meantime was carrying on about what he called 'India's spiritual message', with 'peace', 'harmony' and 'concord' thrown in for good measure.

'But,' said Candide, 'that's rather odd, don't you agree?'

'Why?'

'I've read,' he said. 'Not very well. But I've read—and Indian history always seemed to me particularly bloody. I must have been wrong.'

'But think of Ashoka,' I said.

'Yes, of course, notwithstanding the Kalinga war. Yes. No doubt I was wrong. And all those awful wars. Endless dates to remember. And the dates are either for the death of a king or the birth of a prince or a battle, apart from famines and revolts and other things. No doubt it is human to re-write all this and expurgate the books into something you can read with your children. Most thoughtful of your people.'

'You talk as if we did nothing but fight.'

'It must have been the wicked English who wrote about these horrible battles in your history. No doubt it is patriotic to get rid of all that.' He paused and drooled a little.

We pushed on to the next room. Here, another fat scholar was blah-blahing on and on about how India 'assimilates', if I've got the word right. The country is supposed to have been assimilating without a break since the coming of the Aryans and has already assimilated the Dravidians, Aryans, Sakas, Huns, Parthians, Mongols and sundry other tribes. She has further, without ado, assimilated (what does the word mean anyway?) religions by the dozen. Listening to him, you would feel India was a great big dame with a thousand pockets, and anything she considered worth 'assimilating' she snatched and put into one.

I knew trouble was brewing. And it burst. Candide halted again.

'That, you know, is odd,' he declared.

'It isn't at all,' I said.

'But no doubt you're right,' he added. 'What happened in Calcutta in January is a mere ripple in an ocean of assimilation. And what happened in Jamshedpur and Rourkela is the extermination of vermins not worth assimilation.'

'You're quite right,' I said very fast and would have gone on.

'For example, the Jews in Germany,' he said. 'Odd people. They were impervious to assimilation.'

Things were getting along in a way I didn't care for. But Candide strikes these moods, you know, and then he believes in what he calls 'exploring all possibilities'.

'Another example,' he went on, 'Some of the tribal people cannot be assimilated. Then there is the persistent question of the Muslims. Besides, there is the question of a Bengali in Assam, or a Bihari in Bengal. Other possibilities include North and South assimilation. Not quite assimilated yet. That leads to the possibility of examining the question: who in this case is the inassimilable one? It's all very perplexing.'

'Look, Candide', I said, 'Let's go out and eat somewhere.'

'It is England,' he suddenly shouted.

'What is England?'

'England can boast of assimilation.'

'Oh Christ,' I said.

'Yes. It is quite clear. Jutes, Angles, Saxons, Danes, Romans, Celts. Quite a collection. Can't tell them apart now, can you? That's assimilation. In fact, *mon ami*, any country I can think of in Europe and in parts of America, has assimilated. India is one of the few countries that hasn't.'

There was nothing to it, but to be cross. So I spoke as bitterly as I could of integration and emotional unity, feeling darned awkward and pompous.

'Emotional, did you say? Of course. That explains it. It's all inside you, along with your guts. So naturally we can't see it. It's kind of spiritual, isn't it? *J'ai oublie*—I forgot, *mon ami*, that this is a very spiritual country.'

We stumbled upon a lean, hungry sort of a professor in the next room who talked shrilly of the Qutb Minar being built by the Hindus. He annihilated the distance of time with the irrefutable argument that the Muslims could not have built it because they were not mentally mature enough to do so. At this the house applauded.

'I want to pee,' said Candide, and we left.

(Written under the pseudonym Iago in *Now*, 11 December 1964.)

SHAKESPEARE AND COFFEE

The Sahitya Akademi and the Sangeet Natak Akademi jointly held a Shakespeare Seminar in New Delhi from 5 to 8 December. You can imagine what it was, what it could not help being—a gathering, over coffee, of very respectable and very stiff-necked ladies and gentlemen exchanging clichés on the 'myriad-minded' Shakespeare. A Shakespeare Seminar threatens to become a scholarly affair, and therefore, the first paper was devised very shrewdly to enable everyone to talk right on without the necessity of swimming through the latest findings of Traversi and Hubler. The paper was called 'What Shakespeare Means to Me'. How simple and sweet! Shakespeare must mean something or the other to everyone, and novelist R. K. Narayan actually referred in his paper to the 'significant' interest his cook evinced when he heard that a film called *Omelette* was in town. Nay more, he declares this culinary interest to be no less significant than that of 'the expert who measures Shakespeare metre with a tape'. Furthermore, a paper like this flatters everybody's ego, and Mr Mulk Raj Anand tripped happily through an 18-page autobiography, including the specific stage of his life when he 'began to read Shakespeare as bed-time reading'. Mr Shamlal 'Adib' talked of Siddhartha and Hamlet lumped together, and suggested that Shakespeare anticipated Ionesco. Mr Mujeeb lumped Rumi and Shakespeare together. Mr Umashanker Joshi, when his turn came, launched on a study of Shudraka and Shakespeare. Mr Narle, Telugu author, turned primitive and, probably for effect, repeated Voltaire's charge that Shakespeare was barbaric. Mr Frank Thakordas was such a mass of clichés that it seemed as if he had set out to collect the most-repeated phrases ever uttered about Shakespeare.

But on one point all these gentlemen agreed, robustly and without reservation—the old superstition that one must not look for a consistent philosophy of life in Shakespeare.

MR THAKORDAS. To look for a philosophy of life . . . would, I think, be placing a wrong emphasis.

MR SHAMLAL. He never even tries to be true to himself. He is always true to someone else.

MR NARAYAN. Shakespeare was endowed with a mind so transparent and clear that it never coloured or obstructed the thoughts and words of his characters.

So, Uncle, there you are. A transparent mind which registers nothing; in plainer words, a moron. Shakespeare could not have a mind, surely, if in over 150 sonnets and 30 plays he never expressed it! If only Messrs Narayan, Thakordas and Shamlal had appreciated the labours of Sewell, Campbell, Danby, Dinamov and Wyndham Lewis, they might have refrained from libelling Shakespeare.

The other persistent superstition dogging many at the symposium—in all its sessions—was that Shakespeare was 'a child of the Renaissance'. But to be backdated is no crime. And we really cannot blame them for not being acquainted with the monumental work of Owst.

The session on 'Teaching Shakespeare', intellectually slightly higher, was a study in self-flagellation. Everybody agreed that teachers spoil Shakespeare, and the audience took them at their word and applauded so enthusiastically that some of the teachers present seemed nonplussed.

The third day's subject was 'Producing Shakespeare'. But practising producers were as difficult to spot around that long sepulchral table as the kiwi. Apart from Mr David William, director of the touring New Shakespeare Company (and he did not read a paper, but just popped in to listen) and Mr Utpal Dutt, there were no professionals. Mr Ebrahim Alkazi, of the National School of Drama, started with a blistering attack on the decadent style of production which relies on illusion and magic and, frankly, advocated Brecht's alienation-effect. Mr Utpal Dutt supported him, adding with malicious pleasure that Shakespeare productions in Eastern Europe were far superior to (and closer to the spirit of the original) than the bankrupt performances in Western Europe.

Pandemonium ensued. No one bothered to find out what the other speakers wanted to say; the *bête noire* had been discovered and must now be hounded. Messrs Alkazi and Dutt's insistence on 'the social motivation in Shakespeare' supplied the cue, and, by verbal jugglery, the table was soon condemning the 'socialist motivation' foisted on Shakespeare. An American gentleman (name unintelligible) then stepped in and declared he had had enough of Karl Shakespeare!

When the tumult had subsided, there being not a surfeit of practical stage-workers in the holy synod, the discussion soon turned to defining 'modernness' and 'infinity'. Mr Adya Rangacharya, the Kannada dramatist, in his brief speech referred three times to himself as 'the humble author of 76 plays', the word 'humble' being, in this case, entirely ornamental. The pretty Ms Vijaya Khote gave an outline, rather irrelevantly, of Shakespeare on the Marathi stage, and appealed piteously for someone to talk of brass tacks and to tell her, poor thing, what she should do to popularize Shakespeare in Maharashtra. No one listened because chivalry is dead.

Mrs Mrinalini Sarabhai, the famous danseuse (what she was doing in a producers' conference the Akademi alone can explain), suddenly went tremolo with emotion and made a patriotic appeal for an Indian approach to Shakespeare, that Shakespeare be interpreted by us in 'an Indian way', that a truly Indian theatre should rise. (I was almost expecting her to condemn the Chinese too in an incidental sort of way.) She further declared that Indians can understand *Macbeth* better than the Englishmen because we still believe in witches. To this the Englishmen present, notwithstanding Prof. Gardner's research into witchcraft in contemporary England, gave wholehearted approval. The *enfants terribles*, Messrs Alkazi and Dutt, tried to declare there was no such thing as an Indian theatre form, that theatre was a world-language. Mr David William finally put the lid on the discussion by scuttling the ballerina's theory of an Indian form; he declared that an Indian theatre was a theatre that was geographically in India, nothing more. Habib Tanvir read an interesting paper but in an accent that few understood.

I did not attend the last day's session devoted to 'Shakespeare in Indian Languages' because I had had well-nigh enough. Incidentally, Orissa was represented at this session by Mr Harekrushna Mahatab. Bengal, boasting of a long tradition of Shakespeare translation was represented by Mrs Lila Majumdar, whose undoubted contribution to Bengali literature does not, I am afraid, include excursions into the highly specialized field of Shakespeare. Sunil Chatterjee and Niren Roy are the first names that come to the mind the moment one thinks of Shakespeare in Bengal. Mr Bishnu De's brilliant work on the sonnets might have entitled him to a place at that long last-supperish table.

The gloom that this seminar cast upon all participants was somewhat relieved by Alkazi's Urdu *King Lear*, played on 6 December. The translation by Majnoon Gorakhpuri proved once more that Urdu alone, of all Indian languages, can capture fully the sound-quality of Shakespeare's verse.

The School of Drama's *Lear* was stark, brutal and in the true Berlin tradition. Alkazi sought to capture the age, a merciless age of the collapse of feudalism, and the costume and music helped him powerfully. Om Shivpuri did not look like a pupil at all, but a full-fledged professional. But, of course, the girls failed, and Edmund, the Fool, Edgar, Albany, Cornwall and Gloucester never rose beyond a good school standard. With so many failures, it is difficult to convince the audience, apart from seeking an apology with the fact that the school has no auditorium and no stage but a largish room cramped with chairs.

(Written under the pseudonym Iago.
Now, 18 December 1964.)

CUES

Tenth February was the sixty-seventh birthday of Bertolt Brecht and it was celebrated in an austere, but eager manner by the newly-formed Brecht Society of India. The President of the Society, Mr Satyajit Ray, in a written message, drew the meeting's attention to the revolutionary nature of Brecht's production methods and the keen consciousness which marks his plays. Mr Manmatha Roy, veteran playwright, approaching 70 but younger than many greenhorns, in his address put the question to the audience: Brecht taught us not to whine, but to fight. Are you prepared to do so? He quoted Brecht's lines: 'I am a playwright, I show what I have seen. In mankind's markets I have seen how humanity is traded. That I show, I, the playwright.'

In very clear terms, Mr Roy called India the biggest and most brazen stock exchange in the world, a market where humanity is bought and sold at a pin's price. The time has now come to give up self-pity and idiotic wailing and, following the militant BB, to use our pens like swords, he said.

The East German Trade Representation in Calcutta sent Mr Behrendt to greet the celebration.

Much has been written on Brecht's epic theatre and his alienation effect, very little on the man's virile politics. Touchstone's visit to the Brecht Archives in Berlin has convinced him that he was above all a conscious fighter in the class struggle and only secondly a poet and playwright. That is not to call him a second-rate writer; even his lesser interest produced some of the greatest works of the century. But the attempt by interpreters like Willett and Esslin to conceal, destroy and malign Brecht's political opinions is tantamount to discussing Danton without the revolution. It just cannot be done. Brecht is as inextricably linked to the violent class struggle of our age as are Lenin and Thaelman. If fascism, the communist underground against Hitler and the rise of the German Democratic Republic are ignored in a discussion of Brecht, we will confront comments that we cannot understand. Brecht's challenge to the Un-American Activities Committee that only a Marxist can be a good playwright, his hint in *Kleines Organon Für Das Theater* (A Short Organum for the Theatre, 1949) that only a Communist can be a good actor, his absolute loyalty to the socialist government of GDR—will all become abstruse. But placed in their proper political context, they become the manifesto of a new theatre. This will be openly tendentious, deriving its *raison d'être* from Brecht's firm conviction that in a society split into classes, there cannot be a theatre for all classes and that any attempt to make theatre independent of classes will end up by making it the agent of the ruling class.

Brecht's epic theatre is based not only on the application of dialectics to art, but also to Aristotle's much-neglected thesis of anagnorisis as opposed to the much-publicized catharsis. Catharsis is based on awe and pity roused in the audience; anagnorisis aims at rousing its intellectual sharpness. But while Brecht's epic style can be traced to its Aristotelian origin as well as to the objective acting of Piscator, Kabuki and the Peking Opera, even to Eisenstein and his sub-titles, the influence of Karl Marx remains predominant. Above all, Brecht tried to free theatre not only of its emotional necromancy but of its slavery to the bourgeoisie. He was out not only to rouse the audience's intellectual appreciation of social problems but also to convince the audience that these problems can be solved. He wanted the audience not only to interpret society but to devise ways of changing it. Applying dialectics, he evolved the fantastic, incredible method of representing in the same scene its hopelessness and optimism, its death and its regeneration, its present and its future. In the same character, he could suggest at once its present disintegration and the possibility of its future renaissance. That is why the actor could not be allowed to lose himself in the part; he had a double, a dialectical business to perform, and hence he neded to remain willfully neutral. The origin of this alienation effect is Marxian dialectics.

What Brecht owes to Charles Chaplin is a subject critics should be prepared to handle. It is Chaplin's inscrutable face that comes to your mind when you watch the cool, masterly, uninvolved acting of the Berliner Ensemble. Chaplin and the Ensemble are on common ground when they present characters as well as their own comments on them in an integrated form. No one can say, 'this is all Verdoux,' or 'this is all Chaplin'; one becomes subliminally aware that one is watching Verdoux and Chaplin's commentary on him at the same time. So for Helene Weigel's Mother Courage; so for Eckehard Schall's Arturo Ui. The Brechtian actor is the character and not-character at the same time. That is to say, the dual nature—the present tragedy and future hope—is not presented in a dissected, analysed, guinea-pig form, but together, dialectically, as one artistic whole. That is how the Ensemble keeps its audience awestruck. This is where Brecht's Chaplinesque dispassion makes us aware of the inadequacy of man's higher nature while his cigar glows in good humour.

A man lives by his head
His head will not suffice.
Just take a look at your own heads,
At most supporting lice.

(Written under the pseudonym Touchstone.
Now, 19 February 1965.)

Euler of the Theatre

A Calcutta journalist has chosen to write on the Star Theatre outrage in a Bombay weekly. He thinks that *Ekak Dashak Shatak* (A Year, A Decade, A Century) as it was before it was mutilated was pure 'slander', that it made no specific accusation against the Congress which could be answered. Growing a little more eloquent he adds, 'It advocates nothing, repudiates nothing.' It is obvious that the gentleman never saw the play. Every sentence that the man-in-khaddar uttered in the play and every rejoinder by the others was a chargesheet against the Congress. In fact, it is quite obvious that he has not been to any theatre in Calcutta recently because he rejects Bengali theatre as 'basically hamstrung'. We have a bumper crop every now and then of these unofficial publicists of bureaucracy, whose desire to pass judgement is only matched by their ignorance of the what they judge.

His argument against making a Congressman a brothel-keeper is based on straight mathematics. 'Can it reasonably be claimed that the proportion of brothel-keepers is higher among Congressmen than among ordinary citizens?' he asks rhetorically. Thus it is a simple question of averages. Note also the word 'proportion'. We are instructed to calculate the exact percentage of brothel-keepers among Congressmen. If such statistical exercises yield a ratio of one is to four or some such figure, only then is a playwright mathematically permitted to dress his villain in khaddar. Of course, it is never denied that Congressmen do 'dabble in such trades', but the number is everything! The difference between drama and slander is determined by mathematics!

By the same argument, a Hindu murderer in any play is first to be subjected to a rigorous equational test; if it be found that the proportion of murderers among Muslims is higher than among Hindus, the villain's dress and religion should forthwith be changed. Though, mind you, the statistician grants there are murderers among Hindus.

Applying the formula further, we might doubt the wisdom of making the Prince of Denmark kill his uncle—can it be reasonably claimed that the proportion of uncle-killers is higher among princes than among ordinary citizens? Once again, it is agreed that some princes do dabble in uncle-killing, but the law of averages makes Shakespeare look a decided slanderer against royalty.

I think we are on the threshold of a discovery as revolutionary in literature as Einstein's was in his field. A Calcutta journalist has discovered the exact, impeccable theorem whereby every work of literature and art can be tested. We have at last been given a really objective standard. It is as unemotional as mathematics. We can now doubt Raskolnikov's importance, because the proportion of murderers among students surely gives the Lie Direct to Dostoevsky. Since a large enough number of drunken lawyers who would die for others is an impossibility, Sidney Carton is got rid of. Nay more, Gainsborough may now be judged by the number of boys who would willingly dress in blue, and Gaugin by the proportion of women who change their underclothes for tropical flowers.

Our suspicion that the discoverer of this formula never saw *Ekak Dashak Shatak* is confirmed by his assertion that the 'imputation' (*sic*) of the play 'plainly' was that the proportion of brothel-keepers among Congressmen was very high. Now, we do realize that working out the solution of the world's literary problems through a single universal formula entails much work in isolated contemplation. But surely a visit to *Ekak Dashak Shatak* was also called for. If a visit were paid, various other imputations would also have been noticed. Brothel-keeping was merely part of the Congressmen's numerous social vices, all of which together gave us an impression that much sin is hidden under khaddar. To pick up brothel-keeping out of the entire play (or was it out of a newspaper review) and make it the starting-point of mathematical research is to project one's own personal taste onto a pretty large subject. Iago stabs his wife; but to turn it into Iago's only crime and launch on a discourse on the proportion of Italian wife-killers might proclaim ones own sympathy for the wives but definitely not explain Shakespeare.

If he had only seen the play (before it was cut, of course), our mathematician would have heard a lot besides brothel-keeping, and would have come to the conclusion that the Congressman portrayed in it was a typical Congressman. He fulfilled the mathematical average. So thought the audience. So thought the Congressman who saw it and hastened to muzzle it.

After mathematics, we come to parallels. England is dragged in as an example of governmental interference in theatrical affairs. England is the model, because she is 'the source of the democratic inspiration of all' except Communists. But, of course, England, whose democratic inspiration created Cyprus, Kenya, Malaysia. To support American gas-bombs in Vietnam is naturally democratic. To unleash mounted policemen on Russell and the peace-marchers is per se a lesson in democracy. Furthermore, the fantastic democratic rise of the Beatles and the extremely constitutional transformation of England's boyhood into long-haired gigolos inspire our journalist. He declares, relying on our ignorance, that the 'entertainer' was warned and 'no less a celebrity than' Sir Laurence Olivier had to change a scene. He admits that the original scene had a fully naked woman on the stage; subsequently, the woman had to be dressed. The parallel is complete. If Britain can stop a nude display on the stage, our government can naturally wipe out political opposition. If Britain tomorrow permits the shooting of mad dogs, our government automatically acquires the right to shoot journalists. To an exclusively mathematical mind, there is no difference whatsoever between a nude and a Congressman. It is a kind of $E = mc^2$ that the uninitiated cannot understand.

Further evidence is provided by the 'withdrawal' of the TV feature 'Not so much a programme' by the BBC, the implication being that the feature was legitimate theatre and that it was 'withdrawn' because the English parallels with the Congress minister threatened the BBC with some kind of arrest without warrant. We who do not know democratic Britain so well have always thought that the TV feature was a direct political skit, and that the government played no part at all in its withdrawal. However, we are a gullible public and do not know the intricacies of mathematical parallels, nor the secrets of democratic inspiration.

This Fermat of theatre insists that there 'jolly well should be' a law with which the government can control the theatre. Like Planck's constant *h*, the constant law of proportions must have something to do with this formulation—probably the proportion of literati is higher among government officials than among dramatists. Writing files gives one constant practice; therefore, what is 'right or wrong' had better be decided by officials.

I apply the formula further and contend that there jolly well should be a law whereby journalism can be controlled. The law of proportions tells me that the clerk in a government joint daily writes about a thousand words more than the average journalist. Therefore—QED—the clerk knows better. Literature too, for similar reasons, should be rationed. Though we might then have to forgo some subversive Tagore and left-adventurist Nazrul, there is no doubt that the ennobling mathematical propositions worked out by this particular journalist shall be spared by the censors—which is what matters.

Our Euler will have his little joke. He declares, 'I have probably earned myself a place in the gallery of other fascists.' We know that fascists do not write—they hire writers.

(Written under the pseudonym Iago in
Now, 14 May 1965.)

The Indian Kulturkampf

The winter issue of *Quest* carried a pretty little article by Mr A. Bharati which exposed the persistent but grossly misinformed admiration of Hitler still prevalent among numerous Sanskrit scholars. Mr Bharati referred to a play written by one such 'scholar' (and performed during World War II by students of Benares), who called his beloved Schicklegruber 'Hit-lahren', and Goering appeared whitewashed as 'Gauranga'. The Nazis in this play defeat England and liberate the Indian rishis. Mr Bharati demonstrates how strongly these Hindu traders in spiritualism still feel about their Aryan comrades in brown shirts.

We are at the moment face to face with what may appear to some to be a general resurrection of fascism, and we can date it from October 1962. Prior to that, during the general elections, we had a taste of things to come. It is well known that political parties in West Bengal have for long used street-corner playlets for propaganda, especially during elections. The Leftists can claim credit for introducing a form of propaganda at least as legitimate as slander through the kept press. But, in 1962, showers of brickbats and crackers by well-known gangsters greeted these groups of actors in areas where the ruling party was strong. In places, the resisting populace foiled these Tammany Hall rules; in others, meetings broke up in confusion and women became principal casualties in the ensuing stampedes. The ruling party too had organized cultural shows to boost candidates and, for the first time in West Bengal, some famous artistes took part in them but none of these shows were disturbed.

In October 1962, with the Chinese invasion, a chauvinism of the most degenerate kind raised its head. Faced with an invasion, there was an outburst of patriotism, talks of spirited resistance and national upsurge just as Stalin had done when the USSR had her back to the wall. Stalin reminded the Soviet people that the war was against Hitlerite fascists and not against Germany. Compared to the 200 divisions of exterminating Nazis, the Chinese soldiers who fought us at the border were rather meek. And yet, vicious slogans were raised, primarily by leaders of our ruling party and the nationalist press, repeated ad nauseam by Akashvani and taken up by professional cutthroats and dregs of society. It was always 'the Dragon', 'the Yellow Peril', 'the Yellow Rats', 'the Yellow Pirates', 'the traditional traitors' or those 'who have throughout history been aggressors and expansionists'. No sensible person could help being disturbed by the racial connotation of the entire approach.

The attitude of Akashvani seemed very surprising indeed if one remembers Nehru's statement at the Visva-Bharati Convocation in December 1962: that India had nothing against the Chinese people and their ancient civilization.

The writers of our country—always champions of freedom from totalitarianism—now gave such a display of total surrender to governmental orders as to rival the performances of Pirandello and Marinetti under Mussolini. They stopped at nothing—no abuse was too filthy for China, no invention too blatant. A play declared roundly that China's 6,000-year-old history was a history of piracy. A children's cartoon was called 'The Chinese Swine' (sic!) because they multiply so fast. A play performed in south Calcutta's Mukta Angan described vividly the raping of an Indian woman by two Chinese soldiers—the kind of charge that even McArthur did not have the gumption to make during the Korean War. A leading weekly featured a series lyrically called 'Freedom of the Artist', but actually a sorry confession of the depths these free writers can sink to. Every writer worth the name chimed in with his own views on China, Mao and Marx, and, while first-hand knowledge of the subject was not in evidence anywhere, there was certainly a keen competition to coin picturesque obscenities involving the snub nose, sallow complexion and silken barbarism of the Chinese. Karl Marx, of course, saving his reverence, was outdated, outmoded, moth-eaten.

In this atmosphere of hate and intimidation, our writers and artistes—bearers of the tradition of Zola who just had to listen to Mme Dreyfus's pleadings and of Tagore who threw back his Knighthood like a gauntlet—let down their predecessors rather badly. A famous author, for example, who had written a very creditable book on China and had been rewarded by the government for it, panicked in the face of mob-violence and declared he had penned all that eulogy because the yellow soldiers were holding a pistol to his head; he promised to set fire to a heap of his own books and write a new one on China. Another, a fellow-traveller, promptly reversed his earlier report of the communes of China and declared that they were snares to turn every Chinese woman into an unregistered prostitute. His research led him to the further conclusion that Mao is a sex maniac.

When hysteria rules, disagreement automatically means that the person involved is a scoundrel. Bertrand Russell wrote *Unarmed Victory* (1963) in which he said that India was wrong on the border question. By a peculiar, secretive method, the book was virtually banned in this country but the abuses hurled at one of the wisest men of the century put the late lamented Zhdanov quite in the shade. Russell became 'an old fool', 'a crafty spy of British imperialism' and 'a misguided ignorant dupe of Chinese lies'. Vinoba Bhave was summarily adjudged mad, and hooligans invaded his prayer-meetings to barrack him. President Nkrumah was 'a false friend' and, before long, in the true racial tradition, 'a black serpent'. President Sokarno became 'a licentious hypocrite'. Ben Bella and Ali Sabri were passed over as 'fools', and the indecent, outrageous cartoon on Mrs Bandarnaike was the final word of Bengal's cultural world on contemporary politics. The whole of Asia and Africa seemed to be in a state of semi-civilized existence. India's only friends were the British and the Americans, and our journals and pamphlets were filled with revolting panegyric to the heroes of Congo and Vietnam.

In a race to please the ruling party, the film-makers of West Bengal had the additional task of wiping out the memory of that very moving film on China–India brotherhood *Neel Akasher Nichey* (Under the Blue Sky, 1959). So one director collected a host of stars and singers and produced a work that beat even Akashvani in its infantilism. The reactionary press sprang on Mr Satyajit Ray for remaining silent. While Mr Ray continued in dignified silence, lesser fry made a film with Suchitra Sen as an alcoholic who crashes the border and is shot down by Chinese soldiers. As the Chinese question receded, the Dramatic Performances Bill made its appearance, shaming, by its comprehensiveness, the 1876 Ordinance of the British. It sought to censor not only plays, but pantomimes, operas, *en'tractes*, songs, recitation of poems and all musical performances, thus bringing within its scope even the raga that Pandit Ravi Shankar may choose to play at any soiree.

When the anti-Muslim pogroms broke out last year in Calcutta and the districts, no one was surprised. The stage had been set and the whole act thoroughly rehearsed. The racial superiority preached day in and day out had to tell. Propaganda against Pakistan, always the basis of our *Kultur*, was given a vicious turn after October 1962. People began to see Sino-Pakistani spies everywhere. Militant patriotism had to find a scapegoat and the Indian parallel of Juden Raus was unearthed with indecent haste by hired pen-pushers of the press. Some writers began to spread the communal poison through their short stories and novels.

How has our cultural world discharged its duties to the Nagas? We have through the press, through novels, books, plays, even poems, presented the Naga as a headhunter, a barbarian out to wreck the unity of India. Nagas, being probably Mongols and possessing less upright noses, are not entitled to sympathy, and anyone who shows it to them must be baited.

Crowning this process of feeding the people on hate came Mr Nanda's statement on the Left Communists. Mr Nanda discovered all kinds of guerillas and Chinese arms amongst the lean, hungry and tired lot. He referred to a book on guerilla warfare by Che Guevara and Mao Zedong. Mr Nanda's further reference to pictures hung up being un-Indian was in the true McCarthyan tradition. But most devastating was his warning to those Communists who think India is wrong on the border issue. To think is now dangerous business.

(*Now*, 28 May 1965.)

O Blood! Blood! Blood!

(*OTHELLO*, ACT III, SCENE 3, LINE 455)

There was this nose-in-the-air bloke making a speech. His white khaddar cap bobbed merrily as he went on and on, presumably because he was in love with his own voice. Nobody in the house seemed to listen anyway—nobody except Candide that is, because Candide was hanging on to the blighter's lips as if they were Mlle Chantier's legs in the Folies Bergère.

The bloke said—believe it or not—that India's struggle for freedom does not have any examples in history because it has been totally bloodless. Anaemia in revolutions, he said, was a special Indian quality. He seemed to say—in Hindi, if you please—that Indians are Indians only because they fought the English peacefully. Vice versa: peacefulness becomes real peacefulness only when it becomes Indian. Thus peacefulness is typically Indian. You know the way they talk, switching from A to B and from B to A, until you feel you know nothing at all, that you have always been a dwarf living under false pretences.

After it was finally over, Candide sat glued to his seat in spite of my nudges. When the hall had cleared of the one hundred and seventy-three white caps, he blinked and said, 'That was educative.'

'You're telling me,' I said, 'I feel I'm wearing nothing but my gym slip.'

'That is natural,' he said, 'because all this education can't be good for health. If you consider all the possibilities, a teacher who does not know his lessons is normal in school but he can be rather dangerous when he's grown-up.'

'Ye gods,' I said, 'Let's not explore possibilities. I couldn't care less. I'm not listening.'

'Consider the proposition,' Candide went on, 'that India's struggle against English imperialism has always been bloodless. Apart from the eighteenth-century rulers who fought and died, the nineteenth is replete with indecently bloody examples of Indians who let blood. There were the Kols who fought Col. Adam. There was this zealot Titu Mir who was killed by McKinley.'

'What the hell you are talking about?' I said.

'I'm only trying to tell you that our history books do not agree,' he said, very calmly. 'Probably I am wrong. Your leader must be right. They always are. But then I am always open to correction by leaders. As I was saying—'

At this point I clawed the air with my hands but failed to make any impression and he went on,

'—There was this war in 1857, otherwise known as the Sepoy Mutiny, where a veritable mass of Indians appear to have lost their lives. It was rather silly of them, really, to mess up the history books so. Then of course there were the Wahabis, Faraizis, Sanyasins, Fakirs and things who all died in this un-Indian way. Not counting Tipu Sultan of course, and the Sikhs at Chillianwallah.'

I had faded out. It was the last straw. The man went on shooting strange names. 'The Gurkhas are probably not Indians. The Assam war was rather bloody too. The Maratha war also appears to be a study in bloodletting. The extermination of the Moplahs, Pindaris and sundry other peoples could not possibly have been police action against mere criminals, could it, as the cunning English would have us believe?'

'Are you sure you're not making it all up?' I asked.

'Coming to the present century—' he said, and I felt literally submerged, if that's the word I want. I buckled.

'Coming to the present century,' he said, 'the men that the English called terrorists showed a very special and un-Indian aptitude for lying hither and thither in pools of blood. Some were hanged—of course, they do not count because they did not bleed. The Punjabis and the Bengalis appear to have run berserk at this stage in history and proved themselves unworthy of Indian traditions. Then, in 1942, the peasants in many parts of India went particularly sanguinary, not to talk of the workers who made a habit of being shot at by the police. In 1946, the sailors in Bombay and Karachi also became utterly unreliable and took fiendish delight in sniping at British soldiery and in being sniped back.'

I became vaguely conscious of certain grammatical bloomers in Candide's rigmarole, but before I could poof a syllable he came in with, 'My list is only partial. I have left out a lot.'

'I don't want to hear them,' I said. But then patriotism is an awkward emotion. It doesn't like being handed the raspberry. 'All these blighters,' I said, 'don't amount to nothing. Gandhi alone is worth a million of them. So he counts, they don't. And he was peaceful, poor man.'

'So he got shot too,' said Candide. 'Tragic, really. Just shows you, doesn't it?'

I did not know what it was supposed to show. But Candide came in with what I was terrified all along that he would come in with—'Gandhi is not worth a million Subhas Boses, you know. And Bose's men lustily shot up unnumbered Englishmen.'

Now that was a dirty slight of hand. The bastard was exploiting my chauvinism. He knows I am Bengali.

'There are two possibilities, you know,' he said. 'Either that all these bloodthirsty people were not really Indians at all but probably disguised Chinese—they are everywhere, you know. Or, that their blood isn't blood at all but red paint.'

Now I was angry. I ask you. Really! Was he going to sit there and punch holes into my country? A frog-eater of all people!

'Listen, Frenchie,' I said. 'We never say some people never died. But we do say the real revolution was bloodless, and that was typically Indian. No one else can even think of it. We invented it all by ourselves. How can you understand, you with scalps of the aristocrats sticking out of your reticule? You're Robespierre's descendants.'

'We're always open to correction,' he said. 'But then possibilities arise, you know.'

'They don't,' I said. 'Our revolution is absolutely Indian. That's where we differ from the commies whose flag is a bloody bit of plagiarism, who can't even talk without quoting impossible Russian names.'

'But then,' said Candide, 'where did you find your tricolour except in France? I may be wrong, you know, utterly ignorant. But as far as I know yours is an imitation of—an improvement upon—Robespierre's tricolour.'

This was news to me. 'Are you trying to tell me,' I said, 'that Satyagraha, Non-cooperation and Civil Disobedience are also imitations? You have the cheek?'

'Far from it,' he said. 'I am only drawing your attention to the close similarities in history. Occidental, no doubt. Non-cooperation was Parnell's weapon against Captain Boycott. Though this Parnell had the audacity to precede Gandhi by about 60 years, there is no doubt at all that he must have gone to school in India. And Civil Disobedience is a term invented, theorized and explained by an American plagiarist called Thoreau. No doubt, he too must have picked it up from an old Indian manuscript. And there is, of course, the greatest Indian of all, who taught the world Satyagraha in a barbaric language. In Russian, I mean.'

'Who?' I said. 'Who the dickens are you talking about?'

'Leo Tolstoy,' he said. 'The Indian who spoke Russian.'

(*Now*, 19 August 1966.)

More Things in Shakespeare

Denny sat there, listening to us chat about how our director snooped round to the market every morning and watched people buy tomatoes and eggs. If he perceived they were taking in larger stocks than seemed necessary, it meant we were not going over too well in the town and in the evening we would probably receive the surplus provision, across the footlights in the middle of a scene.

Denny stirred. 'Well, you mustn't play Shakespeare,' he said, 'that's all.'

'Why, is he a kind of hoodoo?' asked I.

'Apart from the fact that the last line of Macbeth invariably lands you in the soup,' said Denny, 'there are more things in Shakespeare than are dreamt of in your philosophy. There was this young fellah in my time—'

'There was this young fellah,' said Denny, 'who called himself Surtees, and our director picked him out of somewhere, the gutters probably, because the blighter had a face. Though it may appear unlikely to you, I was at the time a handsome stripling. If I had played Romeo once, I had played it a hundred times. But I had the disgusting habit of poofing myself in the end every time I played it. What with all that fencing and hugging Juliet and butting into Friar Laurence's middle, soon after the scene with Apothecary, I got thirsty, with the terrifying result that the last scene always lay before me like a primeval swamp without end. I, sort of, groped through. This cove Shakespeare, always likes jazzing things up a bit, and whenever he runs short of "avaunts" and bally emotions, he bungs in a fencing bout. Every night, as I entered Capel's monument, my spine feeling like dough and my knees like somebody else's spare ones, Paris would attempt to apprehend me for a felon there. And, of course, Romeo wouldn't let anyone get away with that. So the inevitable would break loose—yet another round of whacking away with swords. But as I've told you already, at that moment in the performance I wasn't even quite conscious and the balmy bastard on the light-perch would decide to chuck in a bit of atmosphere, which meant Paris was in darkness and I had the screwy spot right in my eyes. I couldn't see a thing, not the tip of my nose. And Paris would, as rehearsed, make the first lunge. But for the life of me, I wouldn't know what was going on if there were 57 Parises all lunging at me with fluorescent rapiers. So, Paris's sword would get me somewhere between the third and fourth ribs with a thud you could hear from North Acton. This would make me shirty and I'd let drive with a swipe that resembled a pull-shot in cricket and catch him, quite taken aback, below the left ear. He would reel, but he was Scottish and he would macmurmur in his ghastly lingo and come back at me in a habiliment of war. For about five minutes, the air would be filled with whirling steel, sweeping arms and Scottish oaths, until the director would be dancing the last number of Petrouchka in the wings, exhorting the uncouth Scotsman to lie down and die so that the story could go on. Just what I was trying to tell him myself, if he'd only let me get a sword in edgeways through the torrents of Gaelic billingsgate.

'This would happen every night. So the director got hold of this Surtees chappie and handed me the raspberry. I wasn't shaken at all because our next play was *Julius Caesar*, and that's one damned play where the young brigade has nothing better than Octavius to do. All these important blokes—Antony, Cassius, Brutus and Caesar—are heavies. They all seem to be married before curtain-up, so that they can plunge directly into murdering one another. Surtees got Octavius, and I—God bless the mark—either Volumnius or Dardanius—I forget which—you know the lot at the end who are whispered at by Brutus and they just keep saying, "Not I my lord." They're somewhat like Rosencrantz and Guildenstern, one can never swear who's who.

'Surtees, being young, thought acting was serious business—silly chump that he was. He seethed with emotion, wanting to make his "mark", as he put it. But with stuff like Octavius you can't go very far— for the simple reason that there are not enough lines. I could see him jogging along onto the stage wanting to saw the air, and then finding there wasn't a bally saw in his hand and coming back to the dressing-room drooling like a thwarted rapist.

'We old hands saw it as plain as the nose on Sol Feinberg's face—storm coming. Hard day's rain a-gonna fall. When you have Shakespeare where even the walk-on talks poetry, and a cove like Surtees, the result is catastrophic. Came Act V, before the battle of Philippi and that mushy little scene where Antony, Octavius, Brutus, Cassius and the impossible names exchange insults, and from my corner I could just see young Surtees wanting to take off. This is Octavius's last scene and he was attempting to concentrate the unsatisfied desires of the whole into it. You know how it goes—as Thingummy talks, you draw your breath in, as Oojacumspiff speaks, you set your face in an immovable grin of contempt, and then as soon as cue turns up you burst.

'Well, Surtees burst on "defiance, traitors, hurl we in your teeth", and as he did so—on "teeth" precisely—we saw something fly—white and terrible—from him, in an arc, shining in the light, and hit an enormous lady in the front row. She screamed, and, looking at Surtees, we found he no longer had a grin. For a grin in the English language you jolly well must have teeth. What Surtees had at the moment was a leer, a hollow, evil leer, an emptiness in the map. His teeth had flown out. There's Shakespeare for you.'

(*Now*, 21 October 1966.)

THEATRE NOTES

Why Classics?

Snobs have always been contemptuous (over their morning cups of coffee, if you please) of the non-professional theatre groups in the city who are modestly building up a movement. Slogan-mongering, puerile, Communist, un-Indian—they have used many such odd epithets. So far, perhaps, they have had some ground—we have been busy too long making theatre a living newspaper and we had reasons for it. But we have also been guilty of neglecting the past, of scoffing at it with silly phrases borrowed from our smattering of Left literature. But now we can throw down the gauntlet. One group is rescuing Tagore from the emasculating chauvinism of Santiniketan; another is rediscovering forgotten classics of the nineteenth century; a third bringing you Shudraka's masterpiece. The classics belong to us and we alone can interpret them for the modern audiences.

Shorn of the classics, a modern repertoire becomes shorn of tradition, rootless and empty. For, the greatest experiment consists in carrying tradition forward, not in denying it; in interpreting and moulding it for our epoch, not in rejecting it as old.

Moreover, the classics give us elemental noble passions that are wanting in contemporary drama. As Robert Jones once said in disgust, 'Modern drama has been reduced to conversation about whether the egg is hard-boiled or not.' There is a tendency in the name of realism to compress the emotions of men and women into the trivialities of breakfast and dinner. The dramatists are busy imitating probable conversation: what would such a character caught in such a situation say if he were real? The result—not even a fraction of complex modern life finds expression in theatre. Life is not just conversation and behaviour, but thought, emotion, passion. Desperate attempts have been made all over the world to capture on stage these other great aspects of life. Tagore heightened his drama from the real to the allegorical. Toller poetized the struggle of the working class. O'Neill's *Strange Interlude* (1928) introduces inner voices of the characters. Brecht tried the epic style with modern themes. Eliot wrote Shakespearean verse about cocktail parties. But most of this expressionist and poetic drama has failed; it has become mere jugglery with forms. It has not the simplicity of the classics.

Why is this so? Because theatre has abandoned its conventions. There was a time when the theatre was all convention. The Chorus introduced the play; the king's chariot was imaginary; Vasantsena's lavish villa was described purely through the spoken word; so was Cleopatra's voyage down the Nile, and the death of Ophelia. There was a time when the actor soliloquized and gave us a glimpse into his soul and not only into his behaviour. What after all is the value of the opera-bouffeish murder of Duncan without that beautiful revelation of a man's soul in 'Is this a dagger?' speech? Hamlet would be a typical Renaissance melodrama of intrigue, murder, ghost, duel, suicide and four corpses to bring the curtain down, except for the soliloquies, the conflicts within a thinker, his struggles with himself, which tone down the horror and give the frantic incidents a new meaning. The Chinese tragedian entered the stage and immediately introduced himself and his problems to the audiences. The Japanese stage manager in black freely walked around on the stage, prompting and helping the actors.

But in 1840 a man called David Hill invented the photograph, and, soon after, the disease of realism gripped the theatre in Europe. And now the Bengali theatre has caught it too. In this country of picturesque gesture and musical language, the dramatists are busy limiting the actor to the appearances of life, immobility and prosaic how-do-you-do's. Would you believe this is the country where the Jatra developed—Jatra, which relies entirely on blank verse and sweeping geture? Would you believe that Girish Ghosh wrote his *Pandab Gaurab* (The Glory of the Pandavas, 1900) and Kshirodeprasad his *Bhishma* (1913)? The playwright today is afraid to philosophize, whereas his predecessor could dare to write in dramatic form a full-fledged treatise on the essential loneliness of man, to express through Bhishma the philosophy of individualism.

Thus, the classics teach us to heighten events from merely a photograph to a full painted canvas. They recapture for us the language of theatre. They show us the methods whereby we may so handle a modern theme that will surprise with a fine excess; it will awe, astound, ennoble. Behind the humdrum incidents of daily life, it will capture the soul of man.

(*Epic Theatre*, March 1995.
Special Commemmorative volume on Utpal Dutt.)

Soliloquy

Edmund Jones left the theatre in disgust because modern drama had restricted itself to problems of coffee-stirring and whether the father likes his eggs hard or soft at breakfast. Gordon Craig resigned himself to a life of solitude and began writing his bitter autobiography. Meyerhold had his theatre shut down. Toller shot himself and Vakhtangov died young. The protagonists of high drama have been successfully dispersed.

And, since the field is clear, the 'realists' hold sway, except for a Brecht here and a Gorelik there. Consequently drama now means whether the boy meets the girl, or the girl chases the boy, whether they lose each other—tragedy—or they find each other—comedy. The characters do not do things, they behave. They do not strangle Desdemona, they merely sigh and say, 'There, now, you've broken up my home.'

The question, however, remains whether this is an adequate portrayal of life. Whether Mr Noel Coward's natural men and women capture truth with the same intensity as Shakespeare's big, larger-than-life heroes; whether *Hay Fever* is more real than *Twelfth Night*.

If realism were merely a photograph of externals, Mr Coward, Mr Ben Hecht and Mr Tennessee Williams would hold their own against Fry, Eliot and Shakespeare. If realism includes man's innermost thoughts, his spiritual experiences, his outlook on life, his attitude (mental as well as expressed), his dreams, his unexpressed desires, then the drawing room comedians of Drury Lane are wasting their time (O, really, Judith Bliss, I love you, but cannot marry you!) and the sooner they quit the legitimate theatre the better it is for all concerned.

Language, today, has lost a lot of its picturesque quality. One does not serenade one's lady below her window, nor are duels allowed. Man has become reticent, sophisticated. It is not fashionable to show one's emotions. It is just not done. The closest you come to saying to a lady that you would die without her is to open a conversation on the weather. One does not fling one's arms about any more—the city is too crowded for that. Naturally, modern drama, true to its pretensions of realism, brings these dull, stolid, silent bank clerks lock stock and barrel onto the stage. And the stage becomes crowded with characters who speak little, express little of what they feel and how fearfully boring it all is!

Now more than ever we should explore man's inner thoughts, and our characters speak out in stirring soliloquies and show their reactions to events and conflicts. The audience has the right to demand awe and majesty and grandeur in theatre, and you cannot give them to it if you limit yourself to the calculative life of the present-day middle class. Before man does anything, there is a long process of thought. What he does is restricted by the requirements of fashion and custom and middle-class ethics; what he thinks is usually free, powerful, primitive and passionate. Modern drama, basing itself on what he does, has become bound by everybody's reality. If it were to invade man's mental world, an infinite variety of unexploited material would come within its view and modern classics be born.

But the howl goes up at once that it would be 'unrealistic' to make the characters speak out their thoughts. In real life, man does not express his thoughts; he should not do so in drama either. In real life, there is no story—life is a continuously advancing process. But drama depends on a story which has a beginning, a proposition, a complication, a climax, a solution. All this we accept naturally in drama. We may, therefore, equally naturally accept a soliloquy.

In real life there are no characters. There is no hero, no heroine, no villain—no punctum indifference. But we accept all these in drama. We might as well accept a soliloquy.

A real drawing room is not open on one side to allow a thousand toms to peep in. We accept this in the theatre. A real room is not bound by hideous neutral wings nor by shabby borders. We accept these in the theatre. One cannot get away from the hard fact that all about the theatre is make-believe. The walls are not of brick, but of canvas and paint; the prima donna's beauty is not of nature, but of Max Factor; the events, characters, emotions are not of life, but imagined, fictitious; and whatever is imaginary must necessarily take on a bit of the fanciful, Disneyish or poetic. And any attempt to create reality in this poetic world is not realism, but a pretence of realism. And pretence has never been art.

Line Rhythm in Theatre

Adolf Appia attacks the two-dimensional picture-scene as a hopeless contradiction. It contradicts the solid body of the actor; it contradicts the floor; it tends to falsify the entire atmosphere. Since then, the painted scene is on the retreat everywhere, and solid rostrums, arches, tapestries, pleated tabs and flight of steps are advancing, filling the stage and pretending to make drama real. But the Appian heresy has not produced its principles, its Bible, its prophets. The previous complacent world of painted garden and perspective royal chamber was an easy one. It overlooked the gross, impossible juxtaposition of live men and dead background, and these minor absurdities therefore troubled no one. But once you begin to clear the Augean stable, you must justify everything you do by means of a principle.

Rejection of the two-dimensional denotes acceptance of the three. If the theatre has to strike out on its own and separate itself from painting, it must resolve this problem of depth—upstage and down. Every element of visual form in theatre must be checked in the light of this individuality—this third dimension. Moreover, there is another more aspect in which the theatre differs from painting—and this aspect has its advantages—the spoken word. Painting visually represents thought without the interference of sound. Theatre bases itself on an audio-visual relationship. We are not concerned here with the intrinsic value of the word, the philosophy of Shakespeare nor the passion in a single speech of Hamlet. Rather, we are concerned with the formal value of words, the metric pattern and their interaction with the visual.

The primary element in all visual art is the rhythm of line. A form must be defined by outline and this outline has a rhythm of its own. In painting, the line suggests movement and mass, apart from defining certain solids. A line can control the spectator's eyes and take them along the desired course. The classical example is El Greco's *Conversion of St Maurice* where the eye inevitably focuses first on the illuminated breastplate of the warrior, then travels along the line of the nude sufferers towards the horizon and then suddenly jumps up to meet the angels in the clouds. Without the aid of a moving frame El Greco has still, within an immovable frame, led our eyes along routes of his choice. Lines can create the impression of motion with the vividness of Delacroix's *Horse in the Storm*.

In the theatre, the rhythm of lines involves the dispersal and arrangement of all visible objects on the stage—from set to actor. With the rejection of the painted scene, the stage, filled with rostrums of various sizes and heights, must suggest a linear parallel of what is spoken. Into this comes the problem of the third dimension. An object placed deep upstage is, from the pure linear point of view, merely a smaller object. Lines are perceptible only on a surface. A line receding horizontally from the spectator's eye looks merely like a point. Dominant in visual art is Euclid's conception of geometry; the later and truer geometry is inapplicable. If the audience's sight-line is to be held the standard, a set's linear design can only be apprehended through a two-dimensional perspective. An object placed upstage may singly be considered 'at a distance', but, from the point of view of line, in linear relation to other objects, it is merely smaller, while an object placed downstage is from the viewpoint of linear relation not 'closer' but 'larger'. Thus the linear pattern of a set can be expressed only in terms of higher and lower, of taller and shorter, and not in terms of farther and nearer.

Three objects of equal size placed on the same plane, but distributed variously—one close to the audience, one mid-centre, one deep upstage—are, to the eye, in one straight line and the advancing line does not exist. The audience sees them in relation to the immovable tall proscenium, and the difference in 'distance' is obliterated. This can be mathematically proved by a simple application of Desargues's Theorem of Papus. If the audience eye be O, and the three lines OA, OB, OC are drawn to the three objects A, B, C on the stage, it can be proved that any three points on these lines—A', B' C' will appear to be in the same line from O. All one has to do is to push these points further from O until they coincide with A, B and C respectively, and it is proved that from O, A, B, C will appear to be in one line. It may not be 'true' in the physical sense. But we are not concerned with such truth in this paper; we are concerned with what the audience sees—and what the audience sees can be geometrically stated in the expressions 10_3 10_3 configuration and 9_3 9_3 configuration.

A friend of mine, puzzled by this impossibility of using the depth of the stage for purposes of linear composition, exclaimed, 'But the thing is actually away from the audience; I can show how far it is.'

But this is exactly why line-rhythm fails. The linear relationship of object and object in painting suggests depth, suggests distance. To go back to El Greco's picture: the line of sufferers seems to recede into the background geometrically; in relation to the figures in the foreground, they are only drawn smaller and smaller. Distance is suggested by a proportionate decrease in size. On the stage, my friend does not suggest this distance; he creates it. His distance is actual and, in proportion to its actuality, this distance is inartistic. It lacks that amount of unreality which is the basis of art. His object placed upstage has no linear relationship with other objects unless they are at the same distance as itself. Using the depth of the stage for linear pattern is a myth.

We see, therefore, that a linear pattern is possible only if the objects are of various sizes, or placed on different planes. With the proscenium fixed, the linear patterns can only be communicated if the void space between floor and teasers can be filled with closely related objects at various levels and of various sizes. An object at a distance can spring into linear relationship with others only if it is raised on a higher level. (Not lower, obviously.) But then, because of the distance, the height will seem less than actual; if the object and its rostrum were to be pulled as they are downstage, they will seem higher and higher. Now we reduce its actual height to that which it seemed to have at a distance, and, as a result, from the viewpoint of linear pattern, it is exactly the same as before. The audience's eye, when engaged in the rhythm of line, never takes account of distance, of depth, and sees the height of an object only in relation to another.

If this relation, this ratio of sizes, is preserved, it does not matter where the objects are placed. What then is the use of the 40 feet of depth lying behind the proscenium? From the point of view of the line—nothing? If the audience were placed perpendicularly above the stage, the up–down linear ideas would be obvious to it. Hence, it is a balcony audience, having the comparative advantage of height over the stalls that have a better grasp of up–down composition. Therefore, we have the producers, never actually facing the fundamental problem, still praising balcony seats as the best. But the major part of the audience sits in the stalls or, worse, closer. Hence, the childish attempt to rake the stage and make it slant towards the audience, hence throw up the distant objects to a comparative height. But if we were to go to the root of the problem, the floor of the stage must stand up as a giant surface before the audience. Nothing short will suffice.

Into this already complicated situation the theatre introduces the living actor, the solid three-dimensional fellow with a voice. We shall now consider the pure linear aspect of the actor's body—imagining him to be silent, dumb (he will create other problems when he shoots his mouth off—of that later). The actor's body is beyond the control of the designer. He cannot à la Procrustes cut the actor down, nor add to his height. He cannot reduce him, nor inflate him. The question of using the actor for linear harmony with the set is an absurd one. Moreover, the principle of linear composition is applicable most severely to the actor, because, given the vast proscenium as a measure, the actors may be considered more or less of equal size and similar appearance.

They appear so to the audience. There is greater difference between a table and a chair than between actors. Hence, the desperate attempts at make-up, at emphasizing certain facial aspects that will distinguish Hamlet from Laertes. As far as general structure is concerned, bar the make-up, bar the costume, they are extremely alike. Structural values being equal, an actor upstage loses proportionately more to the one downstage than if two unequal objects were so placed. The need to obliterate the third dimension is never so keenly felt as when we deal with the human body.

Let us suppose we are trying to create a pyramidal line-structure. Our rostrums, all pulled downstage, rise in severe geometric austerity towards a pinnacle. At the base is a line of actors pointing upwards to the solitary figure at the top. But how long can this composition be held? Drama is not static—it passes on, and a fresh arrangement, a fresh linear pattern, is required. The actors move—and snap goes the pyramidal design. There is a pause—a blank, an interregnum—while the actors form another pattern, a circle or a spiral. Can this be a process of artistic creation—this moving in jerks from pattern to pattern, with void moments in-between?

The moving actor is the principal obstruction to line rhythm. The lines in the theatre are constantly in motion, because the actor must necessarily move. The problem of suggesting movement in a static picture-frame is sought to be solved by moving the masses themselves, by physically creating the movement that is merely suggested in Delacroix. Once more, it is this actuality that prevents it from being art. There is nothing unusual, nothing aesthetic in the fact that mobile bodies move. Art is not created by repeating physical actuality.

Moreover, in a finished work of visual art, there are always dominating principles of line-rhythm. The same principle controls the entire work and inspires all the various compositions and leit-motifs that may spring up and eddy around the main structure. The principal pattern in Beethoven's *Pastoral* is obvious in every movement. Rubens's *Dead Christ* is built around a spiral design. But in theatre, the principle by which the bodies adhere and compose themselves becomes more complex because the components are in motion. One must invent a new geometry of motion before laws of theatre-composition can be ascertained.

Everybody has worked some time or other on the interesting mathematical topic of groups. The process of turning round a rectangle or a triangle along fixed axes produces unexpected result. In this probably lies the solution to unified stage movements.

Let us imagine a pyramidal rostrum with actor A on top, actor B and C at the bases. There can only be a certain number of variations in this arrangement—no more.

1. We can leave this pattern as it is: A as apex, and B and C as the base points. This we shall call business I.

2. A may come down to B's position, B to C's and C to A's, i.e. we turn the triangle round 120° anti-clockwise and the pattern becomes: B as apex and C and A as base points. This we shall call business W.

3. We may turn the triangle 240°, which brings B to the top and the pattern becomes B as apex and C and A as base points. This we shall call business W^2, because it is business W performed twice.

4. A stays where he is, only B and C change positions and the pattern becomes A as apex and C and B as base points. Let this be business P.

5. B stays, but A and C change positions. The pattern now becomes C as apex and B and A as base points. Let this be business Q.

6. We let C keep his position, but A and B change places. The pattern now becomes B as apex, and A and C as base points. Let this be business R.

On examination, we shall find these six patterns are the only ones possible if actors A, B and C are to preserve the dominating pyramidal pattern. If two businesses listed above are executed one after the other, we shall not find a new pattern but go back to one that we could have reached with a single business.

Take business P. Now, on this pattern we perform business R wherein C holds his position and A and B change places. But this we could have got straightaway by business W^2.

Therefore, $P\ R = W^2$
similarly, $R\ P = W$
similarly, $Q\ Q = I$
and $Q\ P = W$

We can go on multiplying our businesses, three and four performed in succession, but we can never get rid of the six basic patterns stated before. If we preserve the principal structure of a pyramid—rather, a triangle in two dimensions, we have obliterated the third—we can have only six variations. Naturally, endless variations can be introduced. But something has gone out—the unity, the principle of linear rhythm. In such a production there will be no guiding pattern, no guiding structure. A, B and C will form all kinds of figures for which no common law can be discovered. Is this art?

But my friend's proposition need not be the only one. His idea of drama springs from his conviction that man is a passionate, three-dimensional creature; and, from a second conviction, that passion necessitates movement. But if he could change this conviction, if he could for a moment believe that, visually speaking, man is a geometric point on the stage, and that a point can have no passion at all, he would agree with me, and find in our triangular composition a thing of beauty. To talk of passion in the actor is to tread on dangerous grounds. We have to rouse passions in the audience—that is the object of theatre. Can this be done only by the actors becoming passionate? Cannot cool-headed patterns rouse the audience's emotion just as well? Let us, therefore, imagine a less passionate producer who is willing to work within a specified structure. Let us also imagine a simple play that lends itself to a simple triangular structure. Movement is automatically severely restricted into six basic patterns with clear linear interrelation among the actors. How then shall we suggest further movements? Only six can be actually created, but many more can be suggested.

Movement in the theatre relies mainly on the movement of the audience's eye. One does not have to rush about in passion to create movement. If it is possible to direct the eye of the audience from one object to another, from one actor to another, and movement, or the suggestion of movement which is more artistic, will have been achieved. The principal weapon our actors A, B and C have is the word. Subject as they are to architectonic discipline, they can still, by exchanging dialogue, draw the audience's eye first to one, then to another. They can create the impression of brisk movement by accelerating the speed of exchange. They can suggest a slow heraldic pace by delayed cues and a longer, more spaced, speech by each character. The word in the theatre has the same function as the line has in Delacroix's *Horse*. Dialogue draws invisible lines along which the audience's eye travels back and forth, up and down, from A to B, from B to C, from C to A.

Once more, a word on the absurdity of depth. If A, B and C were placed deep in the stage, the triangle would become proportionately smaller. In that case, the distance between A to B to C would be infinitesimally small and there would be no appreciable change in the audience's visual line. On the other hand, if B and C were placed at the feet of the proscenial pillars, and A's head were to touch the first border, the resultant wideness would necessitate an abrupt and complete change of the audience's sightline every time a cue is passed on. Even by slightly speeding up the exchange of dialogue, one can, in this case, convey the idea of tremendous speed to the audience.

But this triangle, argues my friend, need not stand up—there is such a lot of space lying behind, so why cannot A be on the floor, upcentre, and C left and right down. But can full use of the word, the technique of passing cues, be made here? As far as the audience's vision is concerned, A, B and C, standing on the same plane, are in a straight line. Passing cues will induce the audience to turn its head only along a horizontal line. How much speed and emotion can be conveyed thus?

But if A stands at the apex of an upright triangle, the audience's head turns not only horizontally from B to C but also vertically to include A. Thus, linear rhythm in the theatre is in the ultimate analysis dependent on the audience's sightline. The lines that connect points and masses are invisible—they are based on sound.

Now the final and most puzzling problem arises—by what principles shall we fix the structure? Will our selection of the basic pattern be arbitrary? Or has it some basis? Can it be purely formal, or is there a relation between form and content?

There is no room in this brief paper for an exhaustive analysis of the visible representation of sound. We have all gone through the writings of Eisenstein and Rene Guillire. We have seen the paintings of Whistler. We may study the image-concept in Indian classical music. We can, if we like, study the metrical analysis of poetry by Edith Sitwell. Iamb and Anapaest give rise to totally different pictures.

It will be enough to point to the austere woodcuts and sketches of Gordon Craig—drawings that grow from the depths of *Hamlet,* they are almost a visible short-hand of *Hamlet*—and to the storm scene design for *Lear,* the whirling spiral drawn across the back cloth that seems to be the leit-motif of the entire tragedy.

It will be enough to quote Jean-Louis Barrault on Racine's *Phedre*:

> The verbal form of *Phedre* is the Alexandrine . . . The form of the actions is circular ; they come one upon the other in perfect symmetry. The total action of *Phedre* is a pure geometric figure.

Let us reverse the process and approach the painters for the element of sound in their work. Gaugin and Matisse and Picasso have all spoken about the musical element in their colour or line. Klee describes the journey of a line across the canvas and makes it the repository of every emotion and sound.

No, I do not think any further proof need be adduced.

Thus, a visible representation, a line structure, can be discovered within the text. There it is possible to subject the entire production to this rigid ruling pattern.

But my difference with my friend brings up the question of the human being as an actor. A production formally based on line-rhythm necessitates the actors being less and less human. They must behave not like normal men in fits of passion but like supra-normal partners in a creation, passing cues—picking up cues and moving with the rigidity of marble figures to form fresh patterns with one another. This 'de-humanization', this attempt to make men look like 'not-men', as well as the attempt to make a three-dimensional stage, springs from a basic urge of art, a basic pretence. All artistic activity consists in camouflage, in so moulding the media material that the spectator will not start studying the nature of the material but will be engaged in what is created from that material. That is the pretence, the disguise of all visual art. When one looks at Hirshfield's *Daniel*, one does not go about testing what pigments have been used, what brushes, what texture the canvas has beneath the coat of paint. Hirshfield has so hidden his media that we forget they exist at all. We are taken up with the biblical 'feel' of the picture.

In the same way, a Chaplin film makes you forget there is a camera working somewhere.

In the same way, any important film creates mass density and depth so that you forget it is really a two-dimensional distortion of reality.

Exactly in the same way should theatre deliberately pretend it is two-dimensional. To reveal its third dimension is to reveal the nature of its media material.

In the same way should theatre conceal the human being on the stage, it should make him look flat or like a bit of frieze or a figure from a bas-relief. It should give him a sculptural look if necessary. But to reveal his humanness is to betray the nature of its media material.

Appia's rejection of the painted scene has been taken too seriously and to ridiculous limits. In extending the sets and the acting-zone backward (away from the audience), we have ignored the possibility of extending upwards. We have created a void, an irritating empty space above the floor. And it has probably been shown by now, that, for the sake of linear rhythm, it is this space that must be utilized to the *exclusion* of depth.

A bold step in this direction seems to be Okhlopkov's production of *Hamlet* at the Mayakovsky Theatre, Moscow. He has obliterated the third-dimension, the depth, and brought his set down almost to the curtain. He has had constructed (designer: Vadim Ryndin) a two-storeyed line of cells, separated by bolted walls. And this gigantic structure rises in menacing proportions precisely because it is so abruptly close to the audience. It is a structural representation of the idea that Denmark is a prison. It is the abolition of depth that gives it its penitentiary atmosphere. Of course, criticism has been targeted at the set submerging the actors (Samoilov as Hamlet), against the actor being 'cramped' and 'static' and, most significant, 'statuesque'. That is exactly why Okhlopkov appears to have succeeded. He has found a ruling structure, and he is not afraid to subject all the media at his disposal to this line—rhythm.

(*Epic Theatre*, March 1995.
Special commemorative volume on Utpal Dutt.)

THE JATRA AND ITS RELEVANCE

This talk will be based on my experiences with the Jatra in Bengal and I hope it will be relevant to the subject in general. Before the current trends appeared, the Jatra, both in form and content, was distinctive.

1. Its content was closely associated with mythology.
2. It was also a morality play, setting forth good and evil in terms of black and white.
3. It relied on the communion of emotion between actor and audience, on the predisposed sympathy of the audience for the mythological hero it knows so well and its hatred of the *asur* (the evil/the monstrous).
4. Thus, though the actor wore no mask, he was bound by such predetermined norms that individual conflicts and emotions did not show up in his behaviour. Effectively, thus, he was wearing a mask.

5. During the great anti-imperialist struggle, new plays adapted the mythological pattern and the British became the new fixed evil and the Indian revolutionary a rigid good.
6. Though songs and dances and stylized gestures did play some part, the Jatra has always been essentially spoken theatre. Even its prose had to be poetic.
7. Perhaps the most exciting thing about it was its clowns and their horseplay, free of religious code; its *vivek* and *judi*.

Commercialism and the greed of the managers of Jatra groups led to a spate of plays which made no attempt to include individual emotions but transferred the entire morality structure to modern conditions. Good and evil now donned modern costume and, shorn of the grandeur of myth, became laughable. Also, the girls began to play girls' parts. The length of performance was cut down from an average of eight hours to three, so that the troupe could play twice or three times a night. Infantile 'experiments' in lighting began, threatening to destroy the actual nature of Jatra. Further, the actors were told to curb and thus emasculate their florid style, and snatches of dialogue began to replace verse.

Over the last three years, however, a far healthier approach is noticeable among playwrights and producers, especially with regard to the subject matter. Politics has now almost swamped the Jatra. Every conceivable subject, from Mao Zedong and Ho Chi Minh to Jallianwalla Bagh, is being tackled, and serious efforts are being made to analyse human emotions in human terms while rescuing the characters from the fetters of myth. But the other and perhaps more important task of reviving the old mythological epics and preserving the style of old Jatra has not been undertaken at all.

While the purity of the old Jatra must be preserved, I believe, new plays and new themes must also be constantly used. The Jatra cannot survive as a museum piece. Its very nature demands that it move with its audience, constantly dramatize the collective experience of its audience. It must reflect today's angst, and yet preserve all that was powerful in the sphere of form, much in the tradition of Peking Opera and Red Lantern.

The problems of production one faces today, if one tries to sweep away the commercial rubbish that has accumulated and create living drama in pure form, are:

1. How to adapt the myth form to modern themes; how to create a fable out of the welter of political and dramatic material; how to be defiantly like a fairytale and yet make it believeable.
2. How to adapt the alienated, conventional and picturesque style of acting to the needs of a credible theme wherein the audience must to a degree identify itself.
3. How to preserve the arena style of production, with its virile rejection of sets, lights and make-believe, and yet create, for example, an atmosphere of total war that a recent Jatra play on Vietnam demands, or an atmosphere of terror that a play on Hitler demands.
4. How to create new verse-drama that will preserve the tradition of old Jatra and yet capture the nuances of modern speech. How to create verse that has to be spoken by an actor and understood at once by an audience largely ignorant, simple and robust.
5. How to experiment but never to forget the source and inspiration of the Jatra—the unsophisticated masses of the countryside; how, at once, to be popular and elevating.

[When Dutt came to address the seminar, for which the following text had been circulated in advance as a synopsis, he had a different text to offer, leading to a lively discussion in which the participants included Ebrahim Alkazi, Satyadev Dubey, P. L. Deshpande, Shanta Gandhi, Dina Gandhi, Suresh Awasthi, Balwant Gargi, Nemichandra Jain, Girish Karnad, Kapila Vatsyayan, G. Shankara Pillai and Samik Bandyopadhyay.]

UTPAL DUTT. I wish to tell you certain things that have been plaguing the Jatra movement in Bengal. I will be speaking only from my personal experience of Jatra and I hope it will be relevant to the subject in general.

Unlike many other traditional theatre forms in India, the Jatra is a living form. It continues to grow. It changes because it is living, and it reflects the aspirations of the people. In the beginning, we had Jatra purely as a mythological subject. We had fixed patterns of good and evil—good painted in white and evil painted in black. In spite of the rather stylized movements, it was mainly spoken drama either in verse or in poetic prose. And although the actor wore no mask, he was considered to be practically in a mask because he had no liberty and no opportunity to portray human emotions or experience, because the story used to be set beforehand. All the stories were taken from the mythologies with larger-than-life heroes like Arjun and Krishna, and the actors who played their part merely reflected the religious enthusiasm and fervour of the audience. There was a predetermined unity of religious beliefs between the audience and the actor. Therefore the norms too were mostly predetermined. Everyone knew the story, and yet they were all sitting together in a community watching their own religious beliefs being enacted, and this would inspire them.

The Jatra has always been not just theatre or entertainment but a school, a court of justice and a political meeting—everything. As the great anti-imperialistic struggle in India began, Jatra immediately changed its character, because it had to be with the people, in the people and among the people constantly. And when the struggle reached its peak, especially in the 1920s and 30s, with the so-called terrorist movements in Bengal, Jatra changed from religious to secular subjects almost overnight and we had historical and political plays. But, significantly enough, the pattern remained mythological. Now, only the actors dressed differently. Instead of the 'good' embodied in Arjun, we had it embodied in the Bengali revolutionary holding a pistol. Instead of the *asur* painted in black, we had the British imperialists. So that although the play was supposed to be reflecting modern themes, the pattern was that of a myth with very disparate roles assigned to each character.

The present trend in Jatra is radically different. Everybody knows what is going on in Bengal. Thus, at the moment, the Jatra here is flooded with guerrilla themes. For example, in the present season we have a play on the life of Mao Zedong and Ho Chi Minh and one on Jallianwalla Bagh. I am mentioning these names in order to show you that the Jatra has been moving continuously with the aspirations of the people.

Those who organize and control the Jatra are called the *adhikaris*. They do not act, they only manage it. Now do you think for a moment that they have become Communist? No. They have realized that this is exactly what the people want. This is the kind of play that will sell. Otherwise, the people will not gather in the evening and sit there for three or four hours. But something is lost in the process. Since Jatra is continuously in transition, imbibing things from the current social scenario, and since the mass of people cannot be lifted to a high cultural level, they become influenced by the cinema or any form of mass entertainment which is poisonous. The people want to see the reflection of this kind of acting, of lighting, of all kinds of effects similar to films but which are alien to the Jatra. These Jatra owners respond most readily to people's tastes and in the process try to kill or have managed to kill some very important aspects of the form of jatra—for example, the *vivek*. The *vivek* used to be a kind of chorus, a singer who used to come on stage at a particular dramatic moment, very much like the Greek chorus. He would sing, almost dance, and go away. The *judi* used to be a group of singers who sat with the audience and acted at a particular dramatic moment. They would also start singing, addressing the actors on the stage. This *vivek* and *judi* have gone, and the Jatra owners keep saying that that is how the people want it.

Jatra plays used to be six to eight hours long, sometimes even longer—12 hours. Now they have cut it down to three hours. But, as I see it, the reason is that they want their troupe to do at least two shows a night if not three, and move from place to place so that they can earn more money. But whenever you try any real experiment, they always say 'these newcomers are destroying the Jatra form.' We (newcomers) are destroying the Jatra form just because we are interfering with their profits. Mr Mathur said, in his paper, that there are many troupes which need help. But the Jatra troupes in Bengal are in no need of help—they can, in turn, help the Sangeet Natak Akademi. They pay their leading actors the fantastic figure of Rs 10,000 a month and provide them with a car when the troupes are on a tour. They need not be helped at all. They have tried to bring film actors into Jatra and they have also ordered the real traditional Jatra actors to 'control' their traditional stylized form of acting. This results in emasculation. We see Jatra actors trying to imitate the film actors and the result is ridiculous. Only some very clever directors get away with it. Therefore, there are artistic problems if we try to use the Jatra for modern drama. But we have to do that, otherwise Jatra will die—Jatra cannot survive as a museum piece; it cannot be recorded on 16-mm colour films and be preserved for posterity. That is not the nature of Jatra. Its nature is the reflection of the moods of the masses to which it must cater constantly. It must not only entertain, it must also teach. That is why the peasant comes after a hard day's labour, and that is why, once upon a time, he used to sit right through the night and return to his field in the morning.

The problems of modern producers or playwrights who want to use the Jatra form are very complex. Whenever I use the expression 'use the Jatra form', I become nervous. You see, there are these 'sweet young things' from the city who see 'alienation' in the Jatra and a little bit of Grotowski. They say, 'How virile, how nice. Let us experiment with this form.' But what they do not understand is that Jatra is not just theatre. It is a concept of life, it is a way of life. And unless they go to the masses and live with them and feel the circumstances that they are in, they cannot ever create a new Jatra form. They cannot take it forward. It is impossible. If one wants to really save the Jatra form and create new Jatra plays, one has to preserve the purity of its form and rescue it from the commercial tycoons who now control the Jatra troupes and the Jatra market. If they really wish to do this, they will have to create a new myth—they will have to create the new poetic drama which will reflect modern reality in a modern fairytale.

And it need not always be as simple as it used to be in the 1920s and 30s, because myth can be very, very complex. For example, Shakespeare's wit is myth and yet very complex. So they have to create this modern Indian myth through modern themes, told with the deliberate sophistication of a fairytale—where the characters are frozen in their attitudes, where the characters express not just personal, human experience but the summarized experience of an entire community.

DINA GANDHI. One technical question. You said that the *vivek* and the *judi* were eliminated and are now dead. But why is it so? Did they not comply with the modern content injected into the Jatra, or were they dropped because of the length?

UTPAL DUTT. This took place before any intelligent person took any interest in the Jatra and the traditional actor. While the traditional actor is one of the greatest actors that I have seen, he is not equipped—intellectually—to fight against this kind of tycoonism, this kind of total control under which the *adhikari* has placed him. So around the 1940s and early 50s, the *vivek* and the *judi* slowly began to disappear.

P. L. DESHPANDE. But the *vivek* has not gone completely. Recently, I saw two Jatra plays and I found him in both. He is the only fairly good singer in the group and he helps entertain the people with song and dance. It seems to me that the *vivek* is often being brought into films too, in the form of a beggar who suddenly appears in a scene and sings a song which is in the nature of a comment. It seems to me that the *vivek* is not that unimportant from the entertainment point of view.

UTPAL DUTT. The person who now sings in the Jatra tries to make the song come naturally as part of the story so that, according to the tycoon, it does not jar. But the *vivek* did just that because, when he came, all action came to a stop. The king used to sit down. Very often, the actor playing the king took his wig off and had a smoke on the stage itself while the *vivek* sang. But what is going on now is cheap entertainment.

QUESTION. But can you say mythology has lost its appeal for the general audience altogether?

UTPAL DUTT. At the moment, no Jatra group has a single mythlogical play. But if someone were to bring it back, the audience might welcome it.

SATYADEV DUBEY. You have stated that the Jatra reflects what may be called the already existing mood of the people and therefore what the Jatra expresses already exists. For instance, if there is guerrilla warfare in Jatra, this is because they have included it after sensing such a situation around them. But is it not possible that, at some stage in the history of Jatra, people may have used Jatra to bring about the situation? For instance, let us assume that there may have been a mythological Naxalite who may have used the Jatra form to generate such sympathies from the people. Has this been possible? Has it ever been done? As it has happened in the West? Would you say that the Jatra has always reflected something which has come into being or that a mood which is already present gets reflected in the Jatra? What would you say has happened? Which came first? On one side you said are the owners who use the feelings of the people—very good commercial sense, I must say—and on the other side are the people who are trying to conserve the Jatra in its pristine form and render it through different types of aesthetic experience which may have belonged to the original form. My point is, if a folk form like the Jatra reflects only the given conditions, it cannot be a 'social criticism' because it is just reflecting the given conditions. But suppose you create a Jatra play and use a theme which has not been used before and in that you criticize the existing society. In doing so, you bring about a change in that society. This would then be a 'social criticism' which raises the point: where does Jatra fit? In which category would it fall?

UTPAL DUTT. I think the question is an oversimplification of the case because both things coexist. There cannot be any demand or direction unless the conditions are created first. People have always created such a condition wherein someone through the Jatra rouses them. Thus it is the people who create that condition. But this does not mean the Jatra writer only reflects that condition. He moulds, he further expands and carries the ideas to the farthest corners of the country. For example, Mukunda Das, the great Jatra writer who went to prison several times under the British and was primarily responsible for rousing Bengali peasants on the question of Independence. Similarly, the tycoon sees there is a good market for such plays. He contacts playwrights. He cannot always control them as they are influenced by the contemporary situations. Nor can he control the directors. These playwrights write plays and the directors create new Jatra plays. But they do not restrict themselves merely to reflecting what the people want—their plays also have what the playwright wants and what the playwright thinks should be. In other words, it is not just reality as it is but reality as it should be, and that further spreads these ideas.

SATYADEV DUBEY. That means ultimately the initiative is with the tycoon.

DINA GANDHI. I think it is the commercial pressures that are reshaping the Jatra. Does it then deserve the name Jatra any more? Is it the commercial pressures or is it the moral excellence or shall I say the moral message which it still succeeds in conveying that points to some morality which still makes it appropriate as Jatra? Or is it degenerating into a commercial melodrama?

UTPAL DUTT. As I see it, as far as form is concerned, a lot of corruption has taken place but the Jatra still retains its features. They have not been able to destroy it entirely. But for the last three or four years, conscious people are coming in who are fighting this and trying to create new content in its pure form. Now, the field is not open to the tycoon to do as he pleases. Now, there's a battle. Now, conscious resistance is being offered and experiments are being done—experiments preserving the purity of form but creating new plays with new content to reflect the current aspirations of the people.

EBRAHIM ALKAZI. As far as the forms are concerned, they are very important and are an integral part of communication. I think the structure of the traditional folk plays is a part and parcel of the meaning communicated to the audience. This is because there are various levels of experience and the audience is taken, stage by stage, through these levels. Now, these experiences are not only at the intellectual but also at the subconscious level. That is why music, melody, dance, spectacle, etc. have a very important part. The sensual element, that is all the senses, are exploited and not merely the intellect. What seems to happen, therefore, is when you pour new content into an old form, the form, of course, gets swept aside. But it is important perhaps to understand, through experimenting, through research, through investigation and through a scientific approach to the whole thing, the validity of this form. I think form cannot be taken for granted and accepted as ritual. One has to understand the significance and validity of the form in the communication of the ideas.

SHANTA GANDHI. We may stress the so-called purity of the form. But is there no organic relationship between form and content? When we talk about letting a tradition live, letting a traditional form live, we must understand that it cannot live as it was in the original stage. It has to develop. It is the new content which modifies the form. Old set patterns or rigid and so-called pure form cannot express this new content effectively without necessary modifications and without losing its force.

UTPAL DUTT. The word purity was used in a relative sense. Purity of form was here used against the impurities being imported. Just as you cannot have absolutely pure Jatra form—pure for a living theatre—so you cannot allow impurities to come in either. It is entirely relative.

SURESH AWASTHI. Mr Alkazi rightly referred to the pressure of new content becoming the determining factor in changing the form and the structure of the traditional drama. But take Nautanki which is similar to Jatra. Nautanki also, for more than a hundred years has always communicated, projected new ideas and new themes of social change. But the change in its form has happened only during the last two decades. Right from the Arya Samaj and Swadeshi movements, Nautanki has always encouraged social currents. But it seems to me that the devastating change in the form and structure of traditional, religious, ritualistic or secular theatre as Jatra, Nautanki or even Yakshagana is because of certain extraneous elements in them. In Yakshagana, because of commercial pressure, they are giving up their beautiful costumes, headgears, stylization, conventions, and making it simple, straight drama. Of course, certain changes in structure and form will come in, but these have to be according to a certain aesthetic scheme. Certain features are determined by artistic requirements and are shaped over a long period of time. Folk forms in different regions have continued to change their formal structures. But these changes in Jatra, Yakshagana or Nautanki have been due to certain extraneous pressures. And what Utpal Dutt refers to as the preservation of the purity of form is perhaps needed where these groups are doing various kind of experiments. I am not using the phrase 'purity of form' just to indicate restoration of the traditional mode. We undertook an experiment at the Bharatiya Natya Sangh 10 years ago: we brought a troupe of traditional Jatra actors and asked them, 'For the last 10 to 15 years, you have been performing with curtains and proscenium. You have your *ranga*, your stylization of movement. Will you do this particular traditional play if we give you only this platform stage? And do it as you have been doing all these decades, as you did 30 years ago?' They did. And when we asked them how it felt, they had tears in their eyes. They said, 'We have enjoyed it immensely. It was beautiful. We have expressed ourselves very beautifully, very thoroughly. But now we have to make certain changes in the performance due to certain other pressures.'

BALWANT GARGI. I am coming back to the basic question which Mr Alkazi posed—regarding form and content. Well, Jatra has undergone various structural changes during the last 200 years. To start with, it was all musical—a hundred songs and no prose. In the middle of the nineteenth century, they found the actors could not sing. So they introduced the *judi*. Their emotions and ideas of the actors were sung by professional singers on their behalf, and they were called the *judi*. They were the 'double' of the actors. This was again a structural change, a change of form. Again, people thought of ways to get rid of them and they introduced *vivek*—initially the abstract *vivek* and, in the 1820s, the concrete *vivek*. So Jatra has been undergoing changes during the last 200 years, in structure, form, conventions—everything. So what purity are we really preserving? If we want to preserve the purity of Jatra, it will then have to become one with a hundred songs as it was in the original. Then the *judi*, the *dohas* and, finally, the *vivek*—abstract and then concrete. I do not know what purity we are talking about. I am concerned with the question of the relationship of the form and the content. If we pour new content into a form which has grown slowly, adjusting itself with the changes, is it valid or not?

SATYADEV DUBEY. As I understood the point Mr Alkazi made, the purity is in question now. I saw the Yakshagana festival. At one extreme was Mr Karnad—who to me, was totally acceptable—and at the other extreme were such forms which, according to Mr Karanth, were mutilations. He, however, did not show us the worst form of Yakshagana which is perhaps the most popular in Mysore! Now I think this question of purity ultimately lies somewhere in the consciousness of an artiste who has, at some stage, experienced the aesthetics of a particular form and who is also very conscious that the aesthetics keep changing as he keeps on pouring new content. Yet, somewhere, he has captured the essence of the old form in his work and tries to project it. So the point now is: at which stage does this aesthetics of the form die out and new artistes like Mr Karanth or individual ones like Mr Utpal Dutt take over?

NEMICHANDRA JAIN. The question of content and the form in traditional arts, I think, is a little more complicated than what we think. For example, the content of all traditional plays was myth, which was shared by the entire community. But is the new content that has been brought in really the collective consciousness of the people? Can it really become the same as the myth? Has it already become a myth in society, like the traditional content was—in its formal structure as well as in its approach to life and aesthetics? The myth was related to the consciousness of the entire society—everyone could share it. I think the current kind of artificial pressure—of the so-called 'non-tycoon' on the traditional forms—tends to destroy it just as much as the tycoon does. The question is of the essential relationship of the experience of society and how much the forms have been able to incorporate it. Whether the pressure comes from the commercial side or from some ideological angle, the results, I think, are the same.

GIRISH KARNAD. I wonder if in talking about the purity of forms we are making enough allowances for communication—forms changed very slowly in the nineteenth century as communication was very slow. By the time outside influences came to settle, it had already been 25 to 30 years. The form, thus, changed very slowly. But in the last 25 years, it is not merely the villages which are changing—we are too. And I think this is bound to happen.

The twentieth-century artiste becomes more and more isolated—I am sorry I do not like the word 'alienated' so I don't use it! There might have been a time in the sixteenth or seventeenth century when a writer could have said quite confidently, 'I'll write a play on the Mahabharata theme and this will express not just what I feel, but at least what my whole community feels, if not the whole society.' This is very difficult in the present situation, and fewer people are able to make this claim. Even in a village, an artiste, due to a particular influence (for example, if he is Naxalite and does not have strict religious convictions), is bound to feel isolated. And when he puts across his ideas in the form of a Jatra play, it is hardly the consciousness of the community.

In a such a situation, how does one decide? Besides, who decides and where exactly does this change come from? In which case I wonder, Mr Dutt, if you are not putting yourself on the same wavelength or level of the 'sweet young thing'?

UTPAL DUTT. I think we have taken on a problem which cannot be solved here, across this table. We have gone to the very root of the question—how much of the traditional theatre is really traditional? And how much of the traditional is actually living till date? Which aspect of it has to grow continuously, which aspect is not a museum piece?—meaning, how much of it is really traditional and how much of it collected from contemporary times and therefore still changing? Now, the aspect of 'purity', in a relative sense at least, has to be adhered to! Otherwise what will be the difference between Jatra and theatre after a period of time? If you say after 10 to 15 years all differences will disappear, well, I do not agree because that is quite impossible. Regarding this 'purity'—we have to go back once more to the question of the audience and to Mr Karnad who says, 'Who decides which is quite right?' There is just one aspect which decides and that is the audience. That is the trouble with the Jatra—the decision ultimately is made by the people who watch it.

Unlike the city theatre, for example, the theatres in Calcutta which in a way also influence the audience, the Jatra has to feed the tastes of its audience. In the villages, although we grant that there is still the existence of the old community order and its solidarity, various class struggles and conflicting ideologies have made forays changing the nature of the audience. But, all the same, the difference between a city and a village audience is that, while the village audience which patronizes the Jatra, which create Jatra indirectly by demanding or setting the norms, is a far more cohesive body, the city audience is divided due to various kinds of ideologies. For example, at the moment the Bengali peasant, as a community, is extremely militant. He will probably cease to be so in five years' time, but now he is seizing the harvest and occupying the land supposedly belonging to the landlord. In Jatra, we have to understand this mentality, understand what the people want at the moment. Therefore, when Mao or Ho Chi Minh come into the Jatra and speak about Vietnam, they speak in a language which reflects the struggle of the Bengali peasant. And therefore Ho Chi Minh, as he is portrayed in the Jatra, may not really be Ho Chi Minh from Vietnam, but rather what the village views as a Communist leading the Bengali peasant movement. He is a myth, a legend. And this myth is ultimately decided by the people who watch it.

All the same, I would say that the experimentalists—those presently studying the abstract theatre arts—die a natural death. But if they go and start experimenting with the Jatra form, they become even more dangerous than the tycoon. There is, nevertheless, the great judge, the decider—the people. Thanks to them, the experimentalists have been driven out; they have not been able to produce Jatra plays. They claim to have learnt these beautiful Brechtian techniques from the Jatra andy are using them in the theatre in Calcutta. But they have been rejected by the masses.

I gave you a very terrifying picture only to show you the danger that the Jatra faces and the problems the modern experimentalists will have to face inevitably. But the tycoon is also being defeated. The star system, for example, has broken down. The film stars, who were directly imbibed into Jatra and who tried a little 'subtle acting', have been successfully driven out by the audience so that the traditional actors, trained since childhood in this form, have come back into their own and become stars once more.

GIRISH KARNAD. There are two questions. First, is the very process that makes Ho Chi Minh a myth for these villagers not adding to and yet at the same time breaking up the homogeneity which you say the Jatra has? Revolutionary ideas, proletariat uprising—which of these is not a part of their tradition? Second—and this is more personal, and affects me as a playwright—you did, I think, confuse the 'sweet young thing' who tries to experiment with the Jatra with the man who sees a Jatra play and goes back to Calcutta to produce a play in that form. I think there is difference. I mean, I am attracted by the Yakshagana form. I write a play, in Dharwar, using the Yakshagana form, because I feel that, for one particular play, it helps me give a form to what I want to say. Now, you'll accuse me of hiding behind the intelligentsia of Dharwar! I am afraid I am hiding behind the intelligentsia of Dharwar—not just for this play but for any play I write, even the most realistic play, because that's the only audience I have. The real danger is to try and be 'folksian'. For an urban man trying to go to the village, the problem of 'sweet young thing' comes up, but I was wondering what your attitude would be to such a man? Would you condemn his attraction to the form for what he wants to say at one particular point?

KAPILA VATSYAYAN. Has anybody done a sociological study of those who go to see Ho Chi Minh, etc.? How many of them go to the Kali temple or subscribe to Vaishnava rituals in their daily lives?

UTPAL DUTT. I think the two questions are interrelated. Karnad asks, whether in trying to bring in Ho Chi Minh as a myth we are breaking the homogeneity of the village mind. And the other question is, whether a sociological study has been done to determine how many of the people coming to watch such a Jatra play go to the temple. Now, let us emphasize once more that, as Ho Chi Minh or Mao is presented to the Bengali audience, it is the 'big mass' which comes in. This Ho Chi Minh is probably not the Communist ideologue, neither is this Mao making his contribution to Marxism-Leninism—not at all. The Mao or Ho Chi Minh, as brought to the Bengali audience, is a receptacle of what the Bengali peasant at the moment thinks and feels. As I said, it is the 'myth pattern'. And it does not preclude the fact that the person goes to the Kali temple and it does not thereby cut him off from the revolution or the revolutionary mainstream of the peasants' struggle. Not at all. It would be completely wrong to say that the Bengali audience, by wanting plays on their daily struggle or on their most terrible struggle at the moment—to seize land and harvest—has already become so advanced in scientific thought that they have rejected superstition. That would not be correct.

KAPILA VATSYAYAN. That is the point. What Mr Alkazi says strikes at the very root of this matter—there might be layers and duality in characters. And this can happen only in a country like India where Mao, Ho Chi Minh and the Kali puja go together. This is where the strength of the traditional theatre lies. And, amidst all our discussions of us becoming secular, we must remember that we are not becoming secular in that sense. Thus, another level is added. That is why this whole discussion is valid at this point of time.

SHANTA GANDHI. Behind any of these forms, is there no creative urge of the artiste, or a group of artistes, to express—through a certain type of aesthetic arrangement—certain ideas? That is also a type of responsibility. Is there not the same creative urge and ideas coming together in the Jatra? Otherwise, why a Jatra play and why not a speech? When you want to talk of capturing paddy, what happens to that particularly beautiful aspect which is there in any artistic creation? Who bears the responsibility of expressing that? Isn't that important?

UTPAL DUTT. I do not see any contradiction between the two. I see that the Jatra playwrights at the moment have to, before anything else, make a living. But after that they also wish to express themselves artistically. There is no doubt about that. Some are more artistic than others, but each one wants to express himself artistically. But with the Jatra circuit and its audience, the Jatra tradition and its myths, it is inevitable that some liberties are curbed. The artiste, however, does find artistic satisfaction even when he is expressing the community feeling rather than his own. I can make the feelings of the community my own and yet express myself artistically. My artistic ego and my artistic expression can be fulfilled simultaneously.

SHANTA GANDHI. I want to bring us back to the question of fragmentation of one's audience.

UTPAL DUTT. We have answered that question. This is how the Jatra would get around the question: it does not present, for example, the new myth in a manner which breaks up the homogeneity or the unity of the audience. On the contrary, it re-creates the unity by emphasizing only such points in the myth which will, at the moment, capture the aspirations of the larger masswa. There are some people who are dissatisfied, but, by and large, the big peasant audience, which actually pays for the Jatra, finds that their various ideas come together in that way.

EBRAHIM ALKAZI. On the one hand, I think there is nothing sacrosanct about any form, because forms have been created through history and through pressure of circumstances. For instance, Kathakali. Therefore, there is nothing divine about form. But, on the other hand, there is a big privilege which is being given to these form— and their sacredness arises from the fact that they have been able to reach a very large number of people on several layers of consciousness. Their sacredness is a result of history, the fact that they have been able to exist over several hundred years, that they have been able to retain their validity and relevance through several generations. The validity of any form underlies the creativity of the person involved and this, together with the meaning of that form, generates, as it were, an electric sort of energy that builds up between the form and the audience. What ultimately determines whether that form has validity is the audience. But, in addition, there is also the work that you create along with the audience. I think there really cannot be anything sacred merely about a form. On the other hand, we must understand that the sacredness of the form lies in the works created.

DISCUSSION FOLLOWING G. SHANKARA PILLAI'S PAPER.

SHANTA GANDHI. You said that Koodiyattam is the production of Sanskrit plays in a new style. Do you mean that the present Koodiyattam is not a continuation of the style in which Sanskrit plays were first produced in Kerala before Koodiyattam came into being? Or is it? It is claimed that Koodiyattam is the only living representation of the style of production that is a direct continuation of the ancient Indian style. Sanskrit plays were produced in a particular style and that style and its conventions evolved at a point of time in our history because of a need. Now, it is claimed, that style continues almost uninterrupted. I am just asking your personal opinion on this question.

SHANKARA PILLAI. I feel that the Koodiyattam is an adapted version of the earlier production of the Sanskrit plays.

NEMICHANDRA JAIN. Mr Pillai has also said that all attempts to modernize traditional plays destroy their innate qualities and their artistic form. I think this is a sweeping statement. We have made an attempt to produce a traditional Bhavai play like *Jasma Odan*. It has been modernized to an extent and yet, I suppose, the inherent qualities and content of that form have been retained. Some of the elements, which were probably alien to that form and which had entered due to other pressures, have been removed and its relevance to the contemporary audience has been brought out. The point of such efforts should be discussed in greater detail. Can we use the traditional plays in such a manner that they become more acceptable to the modern audience, even in the urban centres, rather than remaining confined to the rural areas in the old form?

DINA GANDHI. What do we mean by modernizing traditional forms?

NEMICHANDRA JAIN. There is another aspect in this question which should be considered here. There is an attempt to produce traditional plays in a new way with a certain amount of control and restraint. But there are also other attempts—like, for example, Dina's—of writing a new play and producing it in a particular style. There are, thus, two types of influences. One, a traditional play itself, produced in a different manner, and the other, a new play, written in the style and inspiration borrowed from the traditional form but produced in a different way. The two things cannot be lumped together. The two are of different natures.

SHANTA GANDHI. When Utpal says that the Jatra is used in a modern manner, he means that it has gone through a complete and vital change of form. But when I see a Bhavai actor comment here and there about modern things, it does not mean that he has modernized the form.

UTPAL DUTT. I think the more sophisticated and rigid the form, the more difficult it is to develop. The Jatra being otherwise is easier. The forms Mr Pillai referred to are highly sophisticated. But one should not state that it is impossible to develop a form. Anyone who has seen Peking Opera will realize that it is extremely sophisticated, and yet it has been used in Red Lantern to show Chinese resistance to Japanese imperialism.

SHANTA GANDHI. Frankly, when I started doing *Jasma*, I was not thinking of whether I was recreating it or whether I was making any effort to maintain its purity. It emerged out of a particular set of given circumstances. I do not claim that the way I have treated *Jasma* is exactly as it is done in villages. But I do claim that I have retained or attempted to retain the ethos of that form. There is also a change in the content. This is my own interpretation; it is not interpreted like this in villages. Because I incorporated these changes, there is inevitably a certain modification in the form. For instance, my Rangla has become a link, a much more conscious link than the traditional Rangla was. What I would say is that I was definitely influenced by the resources and acting talent that I had. I did something else with Nautanki. I had the advantage of having people who were Nautanki players and thus did not have to make compromises. So whatever changes were brought about, were brought about consciously.

NEMICHANDRA JAIN. This particular experiment that you did with Nautanki in Delhi. When it was taken back to the region from where Nautanki came, what was the reaction?

SHANTA GANDHI. I didn't have a chance to try it out, testing it in the manner I should have liked to.

NEMICHANDRA JAIN. It was tried on the rural audiences who are used to the same play in their earlier version and, to some extent, they were surprised by this version. Yet, they also liked some of the innovations. It was particularly difficult for the players to stick to this new version. The moment they reached the familiar audience, they had a kind of inner pull to go back to their original pattern of playing. There have been certain other attempts at innovation in this Nautanki performance. But that did not succeed. For example, there was the demand for a particular kind of song or tune. They resisted it. They tried to play the new version as authentically as possible. The reaction was mixed—but it was quite liked.

SURESH AWASTHI. We have been using the term 'modernization', but we have actually been using it wrong; it should rather be 'better/modern/creative utilization'. And this will again depend on one's creative style and urge. For example, when our great authority on Yakshagana, Mr Kota Shivarama Karanth, edits the traditional form of Yakshagana, he removes the impromptu dialogue and turns it into a ballet. It kills the very source of theatrical vitality, and this kind of edited or adapted form is never acceptable to the audience. But I have seen similar experiments with Kathakali or Kabuki in Japan—there have been efforts to change and adapt them for an urban audience. The experiments which are being done now by our playwrights are inspired by the creative utilization that I have been talking about. I would refer to a play by Lankesh—*Parten*—which is very powerful, full of tension and dealing with a contemporary theme. The same play we did in Bayalata—the traditional form, with all the conventions and songs, and it was directed by my friend Karanth who is here. I had a long discussion with him. In one sense, the play lost in time and tension, but it had also gained something in the process. Girish Karnad is using a half curtain in his play *Hayavadana* (The Horse-faced, 1972). This is giving it a contemporary feel and enlarging the space on which the action takes place. It gives a completely different meaning.

K. SHIVARAMA KARANTH. When *Parten* was taken up for production for the first time, many people said it was an ultra-modern and absurd play, and Lankesh considered a playwright of the absurd. But the first part was completely in the rural form. It was a problem for me to integrate the two extremes. I thought it would not be possible. But, while going through it, we had a novel experience. Sangya Balya is in a rural form having very popular songs; it has 12–13 tunes which are repeated. We saw a possibility in the three characters, Kitti, Bitti and Kanti. One typifies the middle, one the upper and one the lower class. It would mean that these were three *shadvargs* (good characters) who come to test Man, who can either be a politician or a professor but one who has a very bad record in life. The *shadvargs* come as dogs. We took them as images and gave them mask-like make-up of three dogs. They have scarves in their hands, because scarves are used in the theatre of Karnataka, and this helps to keep the realistic and the non-realistic characters distinct from each other. And when in the end the real Man discovers that he never had any existence and that his entire life was unreal, he too starts singing like the three unreal characters. But until then, only the three unreal characters sing. The real Man's entries and exits were emphasized with specific movements. Since all the actors were city-bred and did not know singing or dancing, they could not maintain the rhythmic movements. The dance had to be simplified or they would become emotional. One actor, becoming too emotional, fell down one day; perhaps he was dancing for the first time. For us, this was an experience of a total theatre. But some people said this was an experiment for experiment's sake. In theatre, one experiments, explores or exploits; alternatively, there can be all the three things together but it depends upon one's conviction. Ours was indeed an exploration. The reaction to *Parten* was very good, but those who criticized it said the play lost its 'tension' and the climaxes did not build up. At each climax there would be a song and the moment there was a song, people felt relaxed. This relaxation from tension was a new experience, and this was our purpose. If there had been 'tension' in this new form, our experiment would not have been successful. Everything was done to bring about this relaxation. And in the end, when everybody joins in to hit Man, they sing a song. It was a very popular song, which is sung even in *Harishchandra Taramati*. Modern playwright Sriranga (Adya Rangacharya), who never has songs in his plays, also felt that this was Bayalata form.

HABIB TANVIR. The use of the Kuchipudi curtain in *Mrichhakatika* was, of course, functional. My reading of the play led me to believe that, for most plays, Sanskrit dramatists give instructions like 'enter seated', 'enter with the shade of the curtain', 'enter sleeping'. But, how were these entries made? Most available answers are unconvincing because they include some guidelines. But, suddenly, someone thought about the South Indian dance form Kuchipudi, in which important characters enter behind the curtain and then emerge from there. I thought this, probably, was the way the characters in Sanskrit drama entered. I used it and people liked it—it was effective, dramatic. And we chose characters who should be so distinguished by the curtain entries but this was functional.

The other day, for instance, in the television discussion Girish [Karnad] said something about his being selfish with regards to absorbing whatever form suits him. Now that is the very essence of any creative work. You might not use the word selfish, though it is expressive enough. It is a subjective process and you really take in whatever suits you so that you can project it most effectively. In *Mrichhakatika*, it was the folk approach that suited it. One cannot justify it any further. At that time, pundits frowned upon it. But, later , they looked back and said it should be revived. And it was an achievement. As I look back upon it, I do not think I would like to do it in the same manner now. One would not like to repeat. All the same, all those things which he toys with and experiments with goes into the making of an artiste. I might repeat it broadly in the same manner and yet there is bound to be something new. *Agra Bazaar* (1954), I am persuaded to believe, is also inspired by a folk form. Yet the difference between the 1964 and 1970 productions is very obvious. Not only have I revised the text, but there are also many differences regarding the use of music and songs. At the same time, I also feel that my experiences with the utilization of folk forms tells me that whenever I have utilized actual folk players I have had far better results. I have learnt a lot with them than without them. When an urban playwright is thinking in terms of folk tradition and trying to give a folk turn to his urbanized images, he will succeed much better in giving it that slant if he uses folk players. He has a better chance of getting away with it. He is able to transform the form which he chooses, giving it the semblance of a folk form.

Now, the next important thing for me is the assertion that these folk forms must inevitably die. Except that the death of these forms are being brought about in a rather unkind way by bureaucratic attitudes of government set-ups—either in the name of tribal welfare or for rural theatre. We have all seen, for instance, *My Fair Lady*. It is in English folk style. Shaw's classic play *Pygmalion* has been rendered into the folk form and all songs are folk songs. Now, what I am trying to say is that, for whatever folk forms exist in a primitive economy, it is very sentimental to say:

'Let us remain poor because otherwise our folklore will die'. But we cannot afford to remain poor; therefore our folklore must die. We must progress. As we progress and industries encroach upon our rural economy in areas where these forms exist and flourish, these forms change their character and finally die. They die in the same way as humans—they age and die and thus undergo a reformation. But this process is not helped by any efforts of authority. So this is what is happening right now: the tribals of Bastar—where I saw a lot of campaigning for the Hindi language—are looking down upon their own tribal dialects, Muria and Maria. They think that they will give the impression of being far more educated if they speak Hindi. But they end up speaking very bad Hindi and very bad Maria and Muria as well. At the same time, some progress has been made. The baskets and brooms they make are exported much more effectively. So there is more money today but their culture is suffering.

What is actually required is the absorption of these folk forms according to the needs of those individual urban people, with particular inclinations and aptitudes, who seek these out consciously. These merging of the folk and urban cultures should be allowed in such a manner that your urban culture emerges transformed, having absorbed and assimilated the folk forms. Then none will not remain the same. The vitality of the folk form should flow into the veins of the urban culture with the inevitable death of the folk form. Now, this is the premise on which most of us, perhaps even unconsciously, work.

It is only recently that I have come to believe that I too have probably done it: when I got these very artistes here in 1958, to participate in *Mitti Ki Gadi* (The Little Clay Cart, 1958) and again in *Agra Bazaar,* or when I do a play today on the streets of Chandni Chowk. This political play I am doing is, in fact, in a purely folk form. Songs are sung because the purpose demands that it ought to be like this. The validity of this form is also relevant to our political and social endeavours. But for some years I was agitated about it. I was fed up with all the beautiful aesthetics that go into the making of a so-called first-class production—in costume, in music, in composition, lighting, everything—because so many people, the potential audiences, the people who are really alive, who can really laugh, are barred from these halls. That was one thing. Another was that our country, with its social, economic and political needs, requires the middle class, the intelligentsia, to go out and articulate its opinions about hygiene and various other things in terms of theatre and approach the people and guide them. But, in recent years, a strange phenomenon has struck most of the middle-class intelligentsia. For some time it talks intelligently about what is going on in the social and political spheres without fighting shy of the fact that it should express itself, persuade people, give suggestions, mould them. But that is only for some time. I, today, am firmly of the opinion that the traditional theatre forms, the political plays and social plays can be utilized more effectively in this respect.

GIRISH KARNAD. One point: the question of *Parten*. I feel that Mr Karanth is using the word 'tension' in two senses—as suspense and as tension itself. I think, what *Parten* does as a folk play is that it gets rid of the suspense part. It was a play originally full of suspense but no real tension. The whole tragedy was because of the tension; the structure of suspense was brought out effectively. That was really nice.

MANORANJAN DAS. You were talking about Jatras in Bengal. I am from Orissa where we have Jatras too. But they are slightly different from yours. Do you think that your Jatra is popular only because it has a commitment? Or because of the form? We do not have any commitment—we are happy that way. We still think our Jatras are very popular.

UTPAL DUTT. Yes, you see all Jatra—Oriya or Bengali—rely entirely on the masses for support, for their very existence. The Bengali Jatra is at the moment declaring its commitment only because the people have moved somewhat towards militant politics. If tomorrow the people decide that they are sick of this politics, the Jatra will also move away from it. I think, as we have already discussed at length, the deciding factor is people's wants—because the Jatra has to exist entirely among the people, with the people and for the people.

SAMIK BANDYOPADHYAY. Well I have a difference with Mr Dutt on the thesis he made for the Jatra this morning. I have seen most of the Jatras that Mr Dutt mentioned by implication or by direct reference, and the ones which takes up the subject of Ho Chi Minh or Mao are simply bad Jatras. In fact I do not think anything of the Jatra material at all. I saw *Hitler*. It was a very bad production and did not use any of the techniques, form or media of the Jatra. It tried to bring in a crude kind of sensationalism, not the sensationalism that belongs integrally to the Jatra. And the only instance where the Jatra finds a contemporary relevance or meaning is one in which it tries to use a historical perspective in a historical situation. This allows the robust kind of acting, for example in a play like *Samudra Shasan* (1971; renamed Surya Shikar/Hunting The Sun) by Mr Dutt. It is about Samudragupta and his conflict with the scientists who speak for science and reason. A historical situation in a historical perspective—it is this particular form and especially the use of professional Jatra actors, trained in the Jatra mode, which creates something very meaningful and exciting out of that. But whenever contemporary themes have been tackled especially by actors who do not belong to the Jatra tradition; they have just imitated the ordinary professional theatre mannerisms. As for example in those on Ho Chi Minh and Mao and revolutionary Vietnam and others like that. So, the only meaningful use of the Jatra, where the actual Jatra form with the use of music, the intricate mixture of the comic and the transition from one level to another was used, was *Samudra Shasan*—a play which wholly used a historical theme. In fact, a point which has not been mentioned earlier is that the Jatra has abandoned its mythological framework. For the last few years it has been concentrating on the historical framework. The structure now is that of history—medieval, apocryphal or even fictitious—not mythology. We have a feeling that mythology is much more remote than ancient or medieval history. Therefore, I do not think that these plays, merely by using the names of Mao or Ho Chi Minh, are actually making a point or are in any way revolutionary—political or social. The Jatra plays were using certain names and certain elements of history but the essence of this was not being utilized in these plays. Neither were any of the forms of Jatra nor its style of acting used. So, I do not think the importance that Mr Dutt assigns to these plays is there at all.

SURESH AWASTHI. We are in a fortunate position in our country, that bodies like the Akademi do not dictate the survival or the creative utilization of any form. Habib said that he will absorb certain elements from a form which at the same time will die and we should not lament it. But, to me, it seems that there will be an interaction and, in the very process of your absorption as playwright or as director, you will revitalize these forms. This has happened during the last five to 10 years. The moment you adopt a certain convention, a technique from traditional theatre, and give it a contemporary dimension, you give life to that traditional form. Thus the very process of absorption or creative utilization is also a process of revitalization. Not a question of the Akademi or its grants and finances.

SATYADEV DUBEY. Hearing what is happening to Jatra has made me wonder whether there is more relevance that one would ask for from a form which is so alive that Marxists and Capitalists join hands in utilizing it, and the 'sweet young things' are coming in? Where there is a form that has a mass base, it is exploited at three levels—by the capitalist to earn money; by the Marxist for his own propaganda; and by the 'sweet young things' for their own satisfaction. There could be another level, however, of somebody who wants to capture the essential purity of the Jatra form and communicate it. This is just the aesthetic pleasure of the form itself. Now, Bharatnatyam does not make any sense to me but, when I see a very fine dancer I certainly enjoy it. This is also valid. The Jatra, surprisingly, seems to have relevance for all four categories of people. Then there are other forms that may die out. But the work of Dina and Shanta in Bhavai or Girish in Yakshagana may, as Dr Awasthi hopes, revive the forms.

SHANTA GANDHI. I refuse to believe they are dying. They are bound to change, in the sense that anything that is living and growing changes.

DINA GANDHI. But a death is taking place—the death of the artiste. This is very serious. The performers are dying out, dying without delivery. That is where the Akademi can help. It is essential for us to meet and think aloud. Since this is a complex problem, if one works in isolation one does not know what to do. We have to do something about going back to the traditional. We have been trained in Western theatre—we know our own only through books and that too only for the past few decades. We must get to know it region-wise and perhaps meet regionally to thrash out these problems.

MEMBER FROM ANDHRA PRADESH. In Andhra Pradesh and other areas, they have been used by political parties in the past too. You used the word 'tycoon' only for those who use it to earn money, but I use it also for those who use it for their political purposes. Some relevance can be brought to these forms only if it is used as Karnad used it, or as Habib Tanvir uses it. We should not use these forms for our own changes, and in the sense that 'anything which is living and growing changes'.

P. L. DESHPANDE. We may be able to have a better idea if we think in the light of what Buddha said in the sixth century. Buddha pointed to the flame of a burning candle and asked a disciple, 'Does the flame exist?' The disciple was not able to answer. Buddha said, 'The flame seems to be constant, but the material that was there a second ago has burnt out. What you are seeing is constant death and regeneration!' When we think of the problem of traditional and modern theatre in the manner of this flame, I think we will realize that their views are not so irreconcilable.

SHEILA BHATIA. How are things that exist today to be utilized?—this should be the approach. This is because the mode of utilization today is what is called modern; tomorrow, the same thing will become a tradition and thus is it will enrich folk forms. We have talked about the Jatra, I should like to talk about utilization of folk songs in creating a modern opera. Before the Partition, we thought folk songs, with their vitality, honesty and lilt, were capable of expressing the aspirations of the people. Those songs were utilized in various immediate situations. The song, '*Cheenga in Chharinga'* was utilized in lampooning certain social beliefs of society, for example 'marriages are made in heaven', or how in villages the peasant does not really like the woman to be educated. This was a song sung by sweeper women and it took up the idea of processing rice, where the grain falls on one side and husk on the other. We adopted this to mean truth on one side and the false on the other. These songs were then strung together and the items became bigger and later led to some operas which we have done. At first, only Punjabi tunes were adopted, but then we used tunes from other provinces too. I am citing this example to suggest that we should take from whatever is there. As conscious artistes, we understand that these things must be recreated, revitalized, so that they can suit modern society. Whatever you and I have today, the villages will have tomorrow and whatever forms they have are bound to change. When folk singers come to town, they take back certain other things that you and I call 'hybrid'. But you cannot prevent this as long as our villages exist. We, in the city, should also try to use these forms in a new way so that these trends of today become traditions for tomorrow. If you want to use them for some political purpose I see no harm, but the aesthetics must be retained.

ROMESH CHANDER. Apart from three or four producers or writers who have tried to take theatre to the people, for the rest, I think, it exists for the sophisticated audiences who must understand the sophisticated ideas it is trying to project. This seminar would be relevant if these writers could say how traditional theatre is helping them to project their sophisticated views and techniques onto an urban audience which will understand them better. Besides, folk theatre in villages has always been utilized for social comment, but social comment of a very mild nature. I think it was a very conscious effort to keep the criticism very mild in order to preserve the existing status quo. I do not think any conscious effort was ever made to change this order through folk theatre. The time has now come, at least in India, when we cannot wait any longer, when we must use theatre to change the existing order. I am interested in Tamasha or Bhavai being utilized for a particular purpose—is to change the status quo. In fact, we must take a step forward and talk about how we can change it.

BADAL SIRCAR. I am not going to clarify any issue. I was very glad when Mr Chander made the first point. I am interested in that, as that is the question that arises when the problem of a man like me has been posed. This is because I work for the urban audience, not that I want to or because I think that it is the thing to be done but because I have no choice. I do not know the rural audience and, however much I may wish to serve them, I cannot. But I still want to work with theatre. I do not know anything about traditional theatre, I have seen practically no Jatra from beginning to end. Still, I think—from what I have heard from others—that there are certain things which can probably be used in the urban theatre made by an urban man like me for an urban audience. I would really like it if the first point is taken up. But the second point appears to be much more important—the social commitment.

SATYADEV DUBEY. I just want to know: what is this conscientious role which the theatre man wants to play?

ROMESH CHANDER. What is the relevance of the traditional theatre to people like you who are working only for the sophisticated theatre?

SATYADEV DUBEY. For me it has no relevance. When a play is written, I try to find out if this is the sort I would like to do. When I did

Andha Yug (The Blind Age), in 1962, I was hardly into theatre—just three years old. I did not know anything about Chhatisgarhi literature or folk theatre. That play has a lot of folk elements in it and yet it appealed to me and I wanted to do it. But this is the urban man's approach to a play—because he finds it meaningful. Maybe a man who knows folk theatre would have the chorus singing in a different way—I just had it recited over the microphone. That is my tradition. I drew on my experience, which is an urban one, from literature and from things I saw around me. Last year, when I went and saw Yakshagana, I saw something that hit me. I got excited and told Girish that the Bhagavatha can be very useful in a play. 'Go and see a Tamasha. As theatre I find it excellent.' Now, this is the urban man's attitude. The only thing which I can therefore say is that there is one conscientious role which the theatre can play and that is not to bring electioneering issues into theatre. I do not mind a committed theatre, generally committed, but, for a conscientious theatre practitioner issues, of elections should not be brought in.

ROMESH CHANDER. Why?

SATYADEV DUBEY. Let me continue. The second thing—in fact, the one which only theatre or any art form can do for me—is to give an insight, increase awareness. How you utilize that awareness, whether in the form of, say, Sartre or Camus, is again a very personal decision. The third thing, which theatre can do and which the modern theatre practitioner has tried to do, is give aesthetic enjoyment. For instance, if I take up a farce I would not dismiss it just because it is a farce. The point is I may be able to, through the form of a given play, even a sort of Yakshagana, give tremendous aesthetic pleasure and yet only serve the urban interest. The Yakshagana, meanwhile, has deteriorated like all other folk forms. The fourth function is to create the folk theatre of the future.

Today, all the film songs that I took in my plays are a part of my consciousness and have become popular tunes in all the villages. I adopt examples from films where I can prove that a song of folk origin became a film song and lost its folk root and has now again become folk. This is the process which takes place, and I think this is what the urban audience is trying to do. *Adhe Adhure* (Halfway House, by Mohan Rakesh; 1969), hailed today as a great modern play, is going to become a small-town play three years hence. But by then we will have gone into another situation. These are the four functions of the modern or urban theatre and the only roles which the conscientious theatre practitioner can play.

GIRISH KARNAD. I have only one point: when we are talking about the difference of the rural and urban audience, I think we are exaggerating it. I think we take too much for granted and assume that the urban audience is very sophisticated. Ultimately, I think, in India, the values of the urban middle-class audience are actually very little different from the rural ones. Those of us who have been exposed to them, those of us who have read about them, do talk about this difference. Often, in a middle-class locality of Bombay or Bangalore, most people not only have contacts but also their families in the villages. So they follow the same ideals of morality, of living, of aspirations, everything, and this links the two worlds. And secondly—where folk theatre and the question of its relevance come in—in the folk form, many issues do deal with contemporary problems. If I may take my own example: when I wrote *Yayati* (1961) and performed it in Bombay, everyone said it was a mythological play and that most people wouldn't follow the story. But the Marathi audience did not want the story—

they knew it already and responded instead to the situation and issue which was at stake. I consider myself as urban as anyone else and, I think, when we are discussing these two and their relevance, we should bear in mind that the urban audience is not alienated as one usually makes it out to be.

BALWANT GARGI. The same problem of the urban and rural divide. I can speak about Punjab—it does not exist there. Because the Punjabis are totally rural in their heart and manners. Even when you see people lunching at Gaylord or the Chelmsford Club, you may be sure they are excited more by Bhangra than anything else. In rural Punjab, a farmer moves on his tractor with a transistor. I met farmers who said, 'We'll use helicopters to spray insecticide'! In Punjab, therefore, this division—cultural division—of the urban and rural is totally absent. I might look a sophisticated urban, but am really rural at heart. That was a point I wanted to make—this distinction in our society is a bit artificial. Secondly, many people were sharing their own experiences. Well I too do plays, and happened to do one on Guru Nanak which I did with great diffidence because the subject was difficult. But the Sikh community and the Guru Nanak Committee talked me into it. I said, 'All right' and started writing it. And then I got a note, 'Please check that you don't use Guru Nanak's image or person in the play'! Imagine *Hamlet* without the Prince of Denmark! But I made a note of it and went ahead. About four days before the show, I received a legal notice and the Home Secretary called me and said, 'We hear you are showing Guru Nanak's mother and wife on stage. People will attack you. Don't do it.' I was frightened by the prospect of it turning out to be a total flop—because even two people are enough to destroy a production, you know. I thought of the many folk forms that I had seen, then finally for

Guru Nanak's mother Mata Tripta, I used a double, the Pradharni—an actress, who comes and reports what Mata Tripta says and later becomes Mata Tripta, as it happens in ritualistic drama. The actor, for example, in Terukoothu, announces the entry of the king and then becomes the king. In the process, the third person becomes the first. I am only going over some of the instances from my own experiences where folk theatre has turned out to be a great help. This play was an effort to battle with a situation where the community bans Guru Nanak. Here, folk theatrical elements did help in carrying this play in the rural areas of Punjab.

BADAL SIRCAR. I want to stick to the original point. I am interested in the question of urban theatre. I do not know Punjab, but in Bengal there is a lot of difference between the urban audience and theatre and theatre in rural forms. Now, I have to work for an urban audience and I can tell you only about their problem. I admit it's a very narrow theatre and I have no intention of carrying it to the rural areas because it does not address the problems of rural people. So I have no right to carry it to them. I want to take it up from my point—not how folk art lives, or should be preserved or recreated. I am interested in pursuing my type of problems. I use theatre as I have learnt it and probably everybody will agree that the concept of theatre came from the West. We did not really take it from the Jatra form. But now, with the increasing complexity of the middle class, we are searching for new forms because we are finding the 'naturalistic form' and the 'proscenium arch' inadequate to voice our problems. Now, we want to break this tradition inherited from the West. So, while I do not want to do anything for rural theatre, I still want to borrow from the folk form to serve my own purpose. There are many theatre groups in Calcutta. I lead a very humble one. We face so many difficulties—we are in such financial straits as we find that the urban theatre is becoming more and more expensive. So what I want to do is to make urban theatre as cheap as possible and to do that I must do away with sets or lights. I need new techniques. But I want it to be urban theatre for urban people. In traditional Jatra, what appeals to me is that it does not use any sets or furniture. In fact, I think in the past the dramatis personae were not allowed to sit although they did use costumes and some props. In an arena-type of production, doing away with the stage makes it even cheaper. So from that point of view I think this traditional form is important to me. I do not want to write a play in the Jatra form but I want to take these traditional forms and use it in urban theatre. How can I do that?

VIJAY TENDULKAR. I would like to indulge in those folk forms that would suit my needs—I want to find my way out.

MOHAN RAKESH. When we choose this subject, of the contemporary relevance of traditional theatre, there are two aspects to it. But we are discussing only one: how far are modern themes and influences to be traced back to traditional theatre? How does the modern influence the traditional forms? But the other aspect is more relevant to us, and that is: how far are these forms going to influence our writing or our concept of theatre? Mr Sircar has very clearly said that he does not have any pretension to any roots in the rural theatre. He, as a theatre person and knowing his audience to be middle class, says he would like to expose himself to more such forms so that he could evolve a cheaper theatre which he can take to larger city audiences. However, I don't understand why this sort of conscious and artificial exposure is necessary. We are being exposed to our traditions in our daily lives. If I live in any part of India, I am exposed to my tradition right from birth. I have absorbed everything I have been exposed to and that lives in me and, whether I want it or not, that is expressed in my work. Therefore, I do believe in greater exposure. Certainly, it may help us bring about better results. But a decision like 'I am going to use such-and-such form for my next play' or 'I am going to experiment with folk tradition because folk tradition should be used'—that I reject totally. That would not lead us anywhere. If it is unconscious, subconscious and automatic, then it is most welcome but if it is an effort because it is the fashion today—then I reject that.

GIRISH KARNAD. I differ with Mr Rakesh only on one point: I don't believe that one gets to know their importance automatically. In any other art, say that of the musician—however good a voice he may have, one would not consider that he knows all styles of classical music. He may have listened to many but he would require to study. Now, I don't know why a playwright should not assume the same responsibility—of trying try to understand (study) these forms. One may not know what form one's next play needs. But as a playwright, one should try to increase the field of knowledge. To that extent a playwright has some responsibility to get to know these forms.

J. C. MATHUR. Exposure is one thing, choice is another. Exposure has nothing compulsive about it, but it is necessary so that the playwright has a choice. Unfortunately, in India, that element of choice was missing until attempts were made recently to enable the writer to see the traditional forms. It is lucky that a writer like Mohan Rakesh was able to see some of these traditional forms—but how many of us had such a scope? Is it not a fact that many of our generation (of the late 1930s) were influenced much more by what we read of Western plays than by what we saw? Therefore, I see some advantage in tthe fact that the playwright of today and tomorrow will be able to see some of the rich heritage of our traditional theatre. Secondly, India is one of the few countries where these forms are living. Therefore, the opportunity to be exposed to them is not a negative thing but any compulsion would be harmful for the creativity of a writer.

GIRISH KARNAD. I think the best one can do is to try and make things specific. We need to get our teeth into some concrete problem—such as the discussion on Mr Utpal Dutt's work—and then relate the problem to a specific end. If others present here could talk about how folk theatre has affected them and about their work in it, it may lend some sort of a focus to the discussion. This is a question I would like to ask Mr Tendulkar, because he has written a play based on the Marathi Tamasha.

VIJAY TENDULKAR. I can narrate the whole experience. I went to see a Tamasha. I had seen a Tamasha many times before that, but I don't know why that was a memorable experience. After I returned home, my entire process of thinking changed. I started talking to myself as though I were a character in a Tamasha—in that rustic language. And I could see the form coming to me. I felt it right from the next day; even my style of speaking changed. I was so attracted by it that I started speaking with the vocabulary of a Tamasha to my friends and family. I wanted to write a Tamasha, and the theme came to me naturally—my people, the middle, the white-collared-class and the absurd situation in which it exists now. I felt the theme would suit the form because the absurdity of the situation would be magnified by it and thus become more effective. So I used the form, keeping that perspective and angle. It became a major influence for many days. Of course, I was not satisfied with whatever I did with the form. But I shall never forgot the sense of liberation I got after seeing the Tamasha that night and writing one. I feel I'd like to experiment again. The final production did not satisfy me.

SATYADEV DUBEY. What were the special elements that you took from the Tamasha?

VIJAY TENDULKAR. It gave me the feeling of liberation, because I had grown used to the vagaries of my form of writing and was fed-up with them. And here was the technical freedom which I required. I think that was the major attraction. Of course, there was that rustic quality of the form too, in the texture of the language, a special language which I was not used to.

GIRISH KARNAD. In folk theatre, the writer is very much in the background; the script and its poems and songs are merely the point of departure. During the performance, the actor as well as the dancer improvise. In fact, the development is left to the actor and dancer. It seems to me from one performance—although Mr Dutt was caustic about references to Grotowski—that the performance is going to take over, lessening the importance that the playwright has enjoyed during the last 15 years. I think Mr Sircar will also agree to this; he has also been working with the performance aspect, choreographing the whole thing. In fact, the playwright is working towards his own annihilation. The more they become attracted to folk forms, the weaker their position will automatically become.

EBRAHIM ALKAZI. I think this condition—of the playwright handing over to the actors—can happen only in a medium where the actors have been living for generations as part of a tradition. This is not something that an amateur or even a professional, trained in a school of drama, can pick up. I think that the theatrical quality, the capacity to keep in constant touch with the audience and to draw inspiration from it at all stages, is the result of a fantastic amount of experience which goes back generations. You are constantly fed theatrical and dramatic ideas which become part of the material you use, part of your improvisation—not something merely inspired on the spur of the moment. This is possible where the oral tradition is very strong or where the literary tradition interferes with a strong oral tradition. The latter is a very important part of one's over-all education and is a tradition shared by a community as a whole. The common language, which is a part of the popular myth, also disintegrates. This is where the disintegration of the folk form takes place, because it is not only the disintegration of a society but that of the spokesmen of that society too.

There are three parties in any folk form that are concerned. One is the playwright who, as Mr Tendulkar quite rightly suggested, feels suddenly liberated by coming across a form which gives him a freedom which he had not thought himself capable of utilizing. This is really the freedom of all dramatic resources. What tends to happen in 'prose' theatre is that you are merely utilizing one of the least significant elements in the theatre—you develop it in terms of ideas, develop it in the Ibsenite form. But, ultimately, you are bound to reduce it to the realm of naturalism, to the element of mere prose leaving aside the other elements of theatre—spectacle, music, dance—which affect you at the subconscious level.

The second fact that comes in is your audience. We need to find out why a play like *Jasma Odan*—which is a Bhavai—suddenly sets up reverberations all over the country, no matter where you perform. The audience too, suddenly feels liberated.

The third element is the element of the director. I feel very bored with the types of scripts that are sent to me and that I have to produce, because I am not interested in producing plays in the Ibsenite manner. I feel that there are dimensions given to these which already exist in some form. I think Mr Mathur's point was very valid and needs to be taken seriously. This is the only country in the world where folk theatre forms exist—they are part of the living tradition. We should, for our own interests, see to it that they continue to exist, that they are utilized. On the other hand, the playwright should have complete liberty to use a large number of conventions and forms from as many forms as possible. Thus, by preserving the purity of the tradition, on the one hand, and by experimenting on the other, and by working with playwrights, we will hopefully arrive at a dialectic necessary for the vitality of the theatrical tradition.

SURESH AWASTHI. I am glad Mr Alkazi has raised these points. Some of us, while talking of traditional theatre, sound like prophets, saviours, benefactors. We should realize that traditional theatre has been there in its own right for the past 2,000 years, and will continue to survive. Therefore, even the greatest playwright or director cannot pass a verdict that it is doomed. The verdict, if at all, has to come from people who have sustained it through the centuries. Apart from this is the relationship we develop as theatre-workers with it in our own contemporary work. There again, I think, we have to approach it in a spirit of humility, with a desire to learn. We have to do what Uday Shankar did in the field of dance or Shanti Bardhan when he created a great, contemporary, creative dance, utilizing all the traditional dance heritage. Or what Vijay Raghav Rao is doing in the field of music. Hussain is now painting a whole series of Ramayana characters and episodes and giving them a contemporary sensitivity—the characters have never involved us in the manner that they are doing now through his painting. And finally, as Mr Alkazi rightly said, it is not a question of limiting, rejecting or discarding prose theatre, but here is a great opportunity, a vast store house living side-by-side inevitably as part of our destiny. Mohan Rakesh used the prologue in this manner in *Adhe Adhure* only because he is part of this tradition. Badal Sircar, without knowing anything about Jatra, writes a play *Evam Indrajit* [And Indrajit, 1963] which draws upon improvisation, because he is a part of this tradition. Therefore we cannot really escape it.

As Mr Alkazi suggested, here is scope for playwrights and directors because it is altogether a different aesthetics from the (urban) theatre of the last 150 years. With prose theatre—we take a script and it is 're-production'. With a traditional form—whether it is Yakshagana, Kathakali, Noh or Kabuki, it is a 'recreation'. They are rich in conventions and techniques which a sensitive playwright and director could use to enrich his work.

Recommendations

The seminar considered the relevance of traditional theatre in the modern context, keeping in mind four aspects.

1. The necessity of continuing the tradition of this form of theatre into the future by those who have hitherto kept it alive and steps necessary for making such continuity possible.
2. The need for establishing a communication, understanding, rapport and mutual appreciation between traditional stage artistes and the moderns.

3. The need for recognizing that modern dramatic expression, whether in writing, acting or production, cannot escape the environment of the traditional theatre, and for considering the ways in which this impact may manifest itself.

4. The need for the documentation of the material of traditional forms of drama.

Of these four, the Round Table, on the last day endeavoured to put across, in more specific terms, the steps necessary for enabling various forms of traditional theatre to survive and prosper in their own environments. It was felt that barring a handful of forms—the Jatra, Raas Leela and Tamasha—the others are languishing for want of patronage. Many participants at the Round Table made several suggestions of which the following received the consensus:

> Since the traditional forms are essentially local or regional in character, an attempt should be made to introduce the regional form of traditional theatre as a group activity in schools in that area as a part of general education. It need not be a compulsory subject but an extra-curricular activity. It is natural that children from families traditionally associated with these forms will feel more involved. But the point is that if the forms were introduced in schools, the children then will not feel odd in keeping up this tradition.
>
> It is necessary to help the performers of these forms. There have been attempts to this effect in a fragmentary manner by certain groups in the cities who have acted as sponsors or impressarios. It will, therefore, be desirable to encourage urban groups to take concrete steps to help actors, performers of these forms—individually or as a group—from the villages and small towns.

It is necessary to have a small fleet of mobile vans, self-contained, fully equipped and simple to use, and easily available to groups on hire for reasonable rates so that they can move about in their areas and even beyond.

Regional and local festivals should be organized in areas where such forms are particularly popular. At these festivals, a sizeable number of awards should be instituted out of the grants given for the purpose by the Akademi. Such festivals at Udipi have already given an indication of what can be done. State Akademis should be persuaded to help annual festivals of traditional forms of theatre.

Short training courses for the more professional among the performers of traditional theatre also be arranged. This can be done at camps, and will enable the more enterprising and proficient among them to give time and energy for this kind of training.

A number of old troupes are languishing for want of leadership from people with sympathy who know modern techniques. It is necessary to assist such enterprises because the choreography and presentation can improve considerably under a good leader. It is obvious that only such persons among modern artistes and producers who can completely identify themselves with the spirit of that particular dramatic form should be assisted to advise and lead troupes. They should work with troupes, not so much to teach as to become a part of them, and, slowly, and with consideration, enable traditional players to present performances in the modern environment.

It would be desirable for the National School of Drama to present portions of or entire traditional plays in an improved and sympathetically edited form. This would require the establishment of a special performing-cum-training unit for traditional drama at the NSD. Care should be taken to avoid forced modernization of these forms.

There are a number of Noh and Kabuki troupes in Japan that are either maintained by the state or subsidized by it. Subsidy in direct or indirect form is also provided by big business houses. In India, traditional theatrical forms would appear to be a worthy object of assistance by organizations or agencies of tourism development as well as by commercial bodies such as hotels. In this respect, Japan's example is worth considering. The Sangeet Natak Akademi could well take this matter up with the Ministry of Tourism.

The organization of a festival of traditional theatrical forms for particular regions in cooperation with the UNESCO, would appear to be an urgent undertaking with a view to getting a comparative idea of the forms prevalent in the neighbouring countries.

The second category of recommendations referred to the necessity of the rapport between traditional and modern artistes. Several speakers expressed the view that even in the seminar there was hardly any opportunity for the modern participants to know some of those traditional artistes who had been good enough to perform. It was explained that it was not the purpose of the Round Table to provide such an opportunity; yet it was readily recognized that opportunities for such rapport would be very desirable and have indeed been provided at the instance of the Akademi at some of the regional festivals. Such communication between traditional and modern artistes is not free from difficulties, particularly because of the language barrier. However, it should be possible to have as interpreters some of the modern artistes and specialists in the region. It is also obvious that such rapport cannot be established by inviting individual traditional artistes to gatherings of modern ones because traditional artistes might feel ill at ease. The reverse process might yield better results. At any rate, the Round Table thought that the Akademi would do well to go into the details of bringing about such a situation.

The third category of conclusions related to the question of exposure of modern drama to the traditional Indian theatrical forms and the possible formative influence from these forms. On this point there was a lively discussion and naturally, any attempts at forcing the pace of such influence were opposed. It was felt that in any case this is a matter which should be left to the genius of the individual actors, playwrights, producers, technicians, etc. While it is not possible to lay down any standard pattern of the impact of traditional theatre on the modern, it might be useful to provide opportunity to modern playwrights and performers who are interested in identifying with those elements in the traditional forms of theatres and can lend themselves to modern presentation or adaptations. In such a process the Akademi can be of help by screening documentary films, as the artistes, playwrights and producers are themselves often unable to go to the locale to witness these performances. At the same time, the Akademi can organize visits to places and festivals where such performances occur. A beginning in this direction on an individual basis has already been made by the Akademi.

(Based on a seminar on Modern Relevance of Traditional Theatre organized by the Sangeet Natak Akademi, New Delhi, from 19 to 21 February 1971.)